The Art of
Paper Quilling

QUARRY

First published in English by
Quarry Books, a member of
Quayside Publishing Group
100 Cummings Center
Suite 406-L
Beverly, MA 01915-6101
Telephone: (978) 282-9590
Fax: (978) 283-2742
www.quarrybooks.com

ISBN-13: 978-1-59253-386-2
ISBN-10: 1-59253-386-8

10 9 8 7 6 5 4

Design: everlution design co.
Cover Design: Sylvia McArdle, Rockport Publishers
Templates: Sojung Lee

Printed in Singapore

The Art of
Paper Quilling

Designing Handcrafted Gifts and Cards

BEVERLY MASSACHUSETTS

QUARRY BOOKS

CLAIRE SUN-OK CHOI

contents

Introduction

I t was twelve years ago when I first discovered paper quilling in a book from England. The book described how to create beautiful flowers, as well as a butterfly frame, fantastic greeting cards, and colorful floral-patterned boxes that were all made of rolled thin paper strips. Since that initial introduction, my admiration for this art continues to grow. When I first started paper quilling, it was necessary to cut my own thin paper strips. Although cutting strips was tedious work, quilling itself was a joyful experience because I was creating unique artwork. Even as I struggled to place my first paper strips one by one, I was delighted by the result.

My paper quilling started as hobby, but with praise and encouragement from friends, step by step, I gradually was able to produce original artwork. I also started teaching paper quilling at a few associations and cultural centers, which helped spread interest in the craft. My very first private exhibition was held seven years ago; the large turnout was unexpected, and it was the most wonderful experience in my life. Just like that, I started as a hobbyist and turned into a craft artist!

I see it as my duty to help people discover the beauty of paper quilling and inspire them to create their own works of art. This is why I decided to write this book—so more people will discover the charm of paper quilling, as I did.

Recently, quilling has seen its status as a popular art craft expanded. Quilling's biggest attraction is that you can create your own artwork with very reasonable amount of money and time. It is a wonderful hobby that brings much-needed tranquility to our fast-paced lifestyle.

The potetential motifs you can pursue with paper quilling are limitless: nameless wildflowers, flowering trees over a fence, butterflies with flapping wings, and traditional shapes created with the five cardinal colors. Paper quilling is attracting attention because it is a practical art form that can be easily applied to everyday items such as picture frames, cards, gift boxes, and decorative objects.

This book will help beginners as well as experienced crafters learn various paper quilling techniques while using a variety of colors to create unique and lasting pieces. By embellishing your life and spaces with paper quilling you will feel the satisfaction I felt when I first started quilling.

—Claire Sun-ok Choi

History of Paper Quilling

The Meaning

Paper quilling is a beautiful and delicate craft that is created by curling, rolling, and combining long strips of paper.

The term *quilling* is derived from bird feathers, which were used by early artists. Quilling also has a very close relationship to the invention of paper. Paper began with papyrus (made from plant fibers) and further developed into parchment and vellum. Until the eighth century A. D., the paper-manufacturing process was not widely known throughout the world, as the Chinese who had become adept at it were reluctant to share their paper-making secrets. After five or six centuries, papermaking techniques had spread to four continents and paper-making shredders appeared in England, Mexico, and New England. Because paper is the primary material used in quilling, it shared the ups and downs of the history of paper.

The Beginning

The origin of paper quilling, also known as paper filigree, may be traced to fifteenth-century Europe. Around this time, French and Italian nuns and monks began decorating religious symbols and articles with ruffled paper strips made by cutting thin, long strips from the covers of old gilt-bordered books. Some historians insist that this was the origin of paper quilling; however, others argue that the use of bird feathers in the thirteenth century marks the true beginning of paper quilling.

The Glory Years

Quilling spread from England to the American colonies and more and more people arrived from England. In this period, the appplications of paper quilling varied widely. It was used on tea caddies, card-playing boards, and wineglass coasters, and even as furniture adornment. North American quilling artists increased the intricacy of their work by applying seashells, gemstones, and wax-work flowers. With the invention of the papermaking machine in England in the early 1800s, paper quilling reached its prime. It was popularized during the turn of the eighteenth and nineteenth century as a hobby and leisure activity among women in both England and New England.

Paper quilling was taught in early boarding schools and loved by many young ladies, especially in Victorian-era England. George III's daughter, Elizabeth, received a gift of an ebony box and screen decorated with paper filigrees weighing nearly 1 pound. It still exists today. The Victoria and Albert Museum in London has on display various types of boxes, cabinets, card-playing boards, and screens decorated with paper quilling.

The Decline

At the end of the nineteenth century, paper became readily available and the popularity of paper quilling had declined. Unfortunately, due to the fragile nature of the materials, only a few quilling pieces from early times remain today.

The Revival

Since the mid-twentieth century, paper quilling has been experiencing a revival. Along with the introduction of new types of paper and the improvement of techniques, the popularity of paper quilling has been growing rapidly. Additionally, the number of paper quilling enthusiasts has been increasing since British and American paper-quilling associations began active operation. Recently, quilling is being celebrated as an exotic and challenging craft by both experienced and amateur crafters alike.

With the availability of thin, light paper strips—and their limitless inspiration and possibilities—the importance of paper quilling has been revived and it is entering a second renaissance.

Harmony of Spring Flowers
Size: 15¾" × 21¾" (40 × 50 cm)

The Basic Tools and Materials

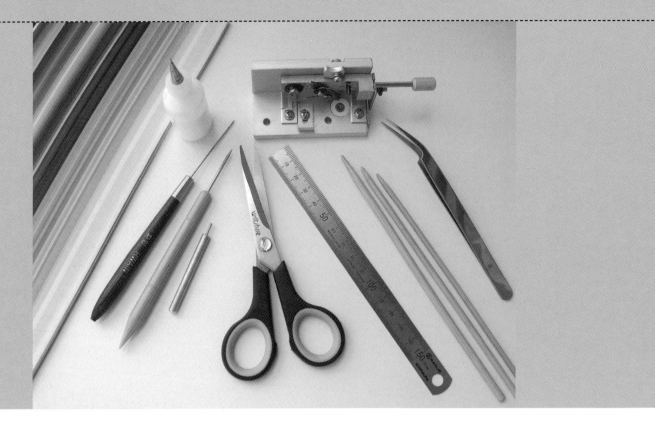

W hen people first encounter paper quilling they are charmed by its beauty, but they seldom have the confidence to try it themselves. However, it is quite easy to buy the necessary tools and materials through specialty stores and the Internet (www.paperquillingart.com). It is not even necessary to buy special tools, as you can use any available tools similar to those recommended here.

Paper quilling is quite different from other crafts because you can start working on simple projects as soon as you have the tools and materials. With a quilling needle tool, colored paper strips, and craft glue at hand, you can produce one-of-a-kind artwork. The items listed on the following pages are the basic tools for paper quilling. Now, let's get started creating lovely paper quilling art!

TOOLS FOR ROLLING PAPER STRIPS

- Quilling needle tool
- Slotted needle tool
- Bamboo sticks of various thicknesses
- Awl

PAPER STRIPS OF VARIOUS WIDTHS

- $\frac{1}{16}$", $\frac{1}{8}$", $\frac{3}{16}$", $\frac{1}{4}$", $\frac{9}{32}$", $\frac{5}{16}$", $\frac{3}{8}$", and $\frac{1}{2}$"
(1.6 mm, 3 mm, 4.8 mm, 6 mm, 7 mm, 8 mm, 1 cm, and 1.3 cm)

OTHER NECESSARY TOOLS AND MATERIALS

- Quilling guide board/work board
- Scissors
- Tweezers
- Knife and cutting mat
- Transparent plastic paper
- Thick double-sided tape
- Craft glue

TOOLS AND MATERIALS FOR DESIGN AND DECORATION

- Graph paper, compass, protractor, pencils
- Straight pins
- Fringing tool

Tools for Rolling Paper Strips

1. QUILLING NEEDLE TOOL

This is a long needle that has a wooden handle. When you roll paper strips around the needle's pointed end, it helps make coiled shapes without any holes in the center. It is also very easy to make spiral shapes with this tool. When attaching very small and delicate shapes, using a needle tool helps you make clean finishes with a small amount of glue.

2. SLOTTED NEEDLE TOOL

This tool has a slotted end in which you can insert a $\frac{1}{8}$" (3 mm) -wide paper strip. This tool helps beginners roll paper strips easily, but it leaves a hole in the center of the coil, which may look a little sloppy.

3. BAMBOO STICKS OF VARIOUS THICKNESSES

By rolling paper strips around a bamboo stick, you can make coils with uniformly sized center holes. Bamboo sticks are especially helpful for ensuring multiple flowers all come out the same size.

4. AWL

The end of a plastic-handled awl is useful for making various bunny-ear shapes.

Paper Strips of Various Widths

In the past, paper quillers cut their paper strips by hand. Today, you can purchase convenient quilling paper strips in many colors from craft stores or online (www.paperquilling-art.com). Paper strips are sold in single-color or multicolor packages. Choose whichever kind is more suited to your project. The most commonly used paper strip widths are $1/8$" (3 mm) and $1/16$" (1.6 mm), but wider widths are also available for different types of quill work. The length and the quality of paper strips varies by brand, so it is very important to take care to choose good-quality paper.

In this book, 10 $5/8$" (27 cm) -long strips are used. Divide these strips into $1/2$, $1/3$, $1/4$, and $1/5$ lengths. Using this method, it is easy to pick out the desired-length strip without using a ruler. To prevent creasing or mixing different colored paper strips together, store them in separate clear plastic bags. This way, it will be simple to find the right colors and lengths for your projects, as well as quickly organize and store your left-over supplies.

1. $1/16$" (1.6 MM) -WIDE PAPER STRIP

Used to make small flowers or flower centers. When a $1/16$" (1.6 mm) -wide paper strip is not available, cut a $1/8$" (3 mm) -long paper strip in half lengthwise.

2. $1/8$" (3 MM) -WIDE PAPER STRIP

$1/8$" (3 mm) -wide paper strips are the most commonly used width in paper quilling. It is possible to roll these strips with your fingers without the help of a quilling tool.

3. $3/16$", $1/4$", $9/32$", $5/16$", $3/8$", AND $1/2$" -WIDE PAPER STRIPS (4.8 MM, 6 MM, 7 MM, 8 MM, 1 CM, AND 1.3 CM)

Wider-width paper strips are useful when making flower fringes, twisted loops, or leaves, and cutting or folding roses.

Other Necessary Tools and Materials

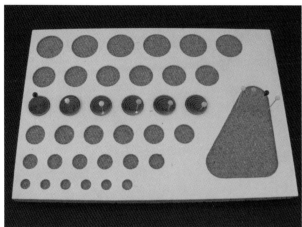

1. QUILLING BOARD/WORK BOARD

A quilling board consists of a corkboard base with a plastic template of six different-size circle cutouts, plus a triangular area for storing straight pins. In addition to helping you coil the paper into circles, the circular cutouts are also used for making consistently sized eccentric shapes. These shapes are formed by placing a loose coil inside a circle, moving the center of the coil to one side as desired, using a straight pin, and then gluing it into place. However, because of the difficulty of maintaining the same tension from start to finish when rolling coils, it is not always easy to make a quantity of uniform eccentric shapes even with the help of the molds.

2. SCISSORS

Small, sharp-pointed scissors are suitable for cutting paper strips, making leaf shapes made from wider strips, and stylizing the leaf edges. Scissors are also used to fringe flowers.

3. TWEEZERS

Tweezers should have long and pointy tips, and the ends should be curved. These are easier to use than straight-end tweezers. Tweezers are essential tool for picking up small parts and rolling paper strips, so they should be clean, easy to handle, and light.

4. KNIFE, CUTTING MAT, AND METAL RULER

These tools are used when you cut your own paper strips. Place a sheet of the desired color paper on the cutting board and place a piece of graph paper on top of it. Because the measurements are already marked on the graph paper, you can save time by cutting the two pieces of paper together. Use extra caution when using craft knives as they are very sharp and dangerous. Also, remember to always use a metal ruler, preferably of stainless steel, as the knife will pare away a plastic ruler (and even eventually, an aluminum one), rendering it useless.

5. Transparent Plastic Paper/Tracing Paper

Placing a sheet of transparent plastic paper or tracing paper on the work board makes gathering and gluing parts together easier.

6. Thick Double-Sided Tape/Clear Plastic Tape

Thick double-sided tape can be used as a base when you desire to create a three-dimensional look. It also has a decorative use, as you can stick paper to the tape and cut triangular or square shapes. Clear plastic tape is used to fix paper pieces in place.

7. Craft Glue

White craft glue is essential for paper quilling. This glue tends to dry fast, so squeeze out only a small amount onto a piece of paper. Nowadays, you can purchase a very small glue container or one that has a very small opening. These specially designed containers with very small openings eliminate the need for a needle tool or pin to apply glue.

Tools and Materials for Design and Decoration

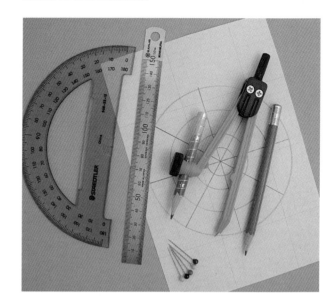

1. Graph Paper, Compass, Protractor, and Pencils

Graph paper is useful for drawing geometrical shapes and cutting $\frac{1}{8}$", $\frac{1}{4}$", $\frac{5}{16}$", and $\frac{3}{8}$" (3 mm, 6 mm, 8 mm, and 1 cm) -wide strips. You can also use it when making basket shapes. A protractor, compass, and pencil are useful for making snowflake patterns. You can make various types of flowers and snowflakes by marking the center of a piece of graph paper, drawing concentric circles, then drawing several lines through the center of the circle.

2. Straight Pins

After a loose coil is placed into a circle cutout, straight pins are used to position the center to one side. Straight pins are also useful when making loop or fan huskings.

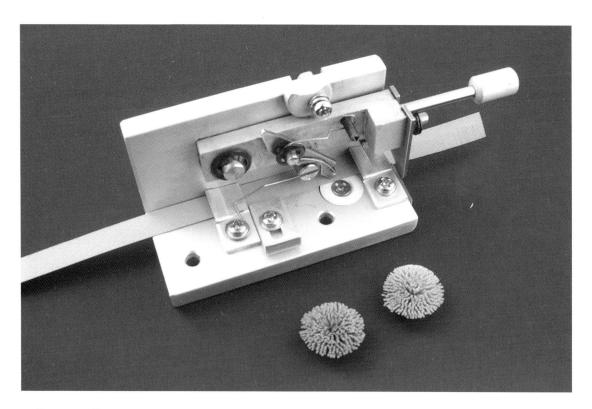

3. FRINGING TOOL

You can make fringes by cutting one side of wide paper strips—$\frac{1}{4}$", $\frac{5}{16}$", and $\frac{3}{8}$" (6 mm, 8 mm, and 1 cm)—with scissors. A fringing machine can help you cut uniform-width strips. This machine may be used to cut $\frac{1}{4}$", $\frac{5}{16}$", and $\frac{3}{8}$" (6 mm, 8 mm, and 1 cm) -wide paper strips; however, $\frac{1}{8}$" (3 mm) and $\frac{1}{2}$" (1.3 cm) -wide strips should be cut by hand. A fringing machine may be purchased from paper quilling stores or online, but they are expensive.

ONLINE RESOURCES - - - - - - - - - - - - - - - - -

www.naqg.org
www.quilling-guild.co.uk
www.paperquillingart.com

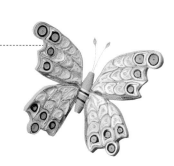

Basic Shapes and Techniques

The basic quilling shapes consist of rolls, scrolls, eccentric rolls, and other irregular shapes designed by crafters. This book contains forty-five basic configurations made by using ⅛" (3 mm) -wide by 10⅝" (27 cm) -long paper strips. The projects that they are used for will be novel, but don't be intimidated! Now, let's start practicing the basic shapes and applying them to your own unique and wonderful quill work.

Roll Shapes

1. TIGHT ROLL

The tight roll is one of the basic shapes in paper quilling. It can be used as the center of a flower or it can be a flower itself. Hold one end of a paper strip with your thumb and index finger, and place a needle tool on the end of the strip. Press the paper strip against the needle tool and start rolling it up tightly. After rolling one-third of the strip, take out the needle tool and continue rolling the remainder of the strip with your fingers. Glue down the end of the paper. If you do not have a needle tool, you can roll the paper strips using your fingers. First, soften one end of the paper by rubbing it with your fingertips and then start rolling. When you roll with your fingers you must hold the roll together with your other hand so that it does not become loose.

2. TIGHT ROLL WITH A CENTER HOLE

Roll a paper strip around a bamboo stick and glue the end.

3. TIGHT TEARDROP WITH A CENTER HOLE

Roll a paper strip around a bamboo stick and glue the end. Form a teardrop shape by pinching one end to form a point.

4. TIGHT MARQUISE WITH A CENTER HOLE

Roll a paper strip around a stick to form a tight roll and glue the end. Press the middle of the roll to form an oval shape.

5. TIGHT MARQUISE WITH CENTER SPACES

Roll half the length of a paper strip, then form an oval-shaped roll. Continue rolling the remainder of the strip tightly to make an oval shape.

6. TIGHT ROLL WITH CENTER SPACES

Roll half the length of a paper strip to form a loose roll. Continue rolling the remainder of the strip tightly to form a tight roll.

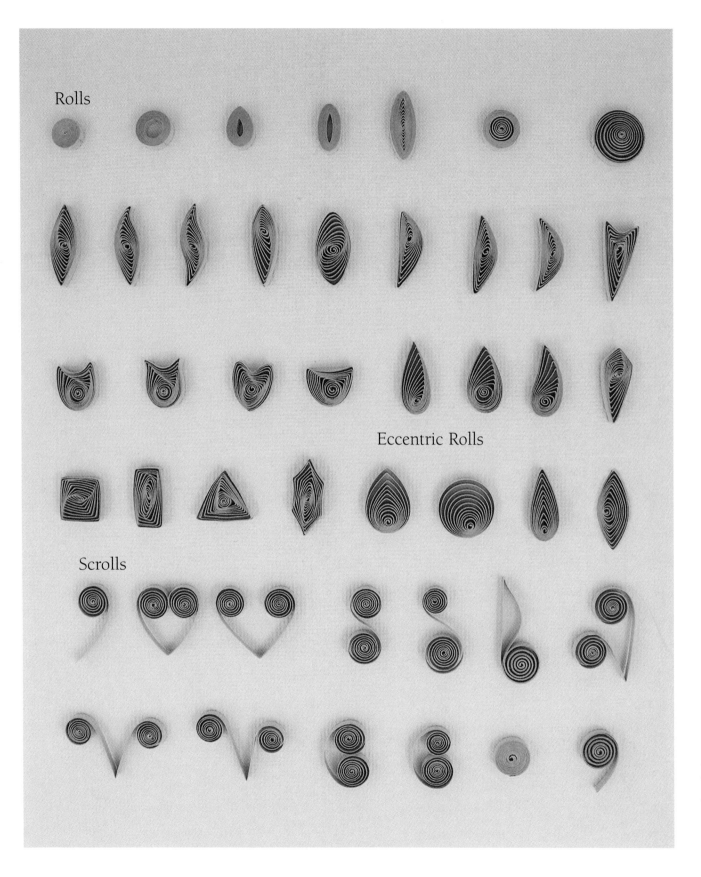

Rolls

Eccentric Rolls

Scrolls

7. LOOSE COIL

Loosen a tight coil to the desired size. To make a uniformly spaced coil, you must maintain the same tension from start to finish when rolling the coil. If you make a mistake, unroll the strip and repeat the steps. This loose coil is the first step in making the following basic paper quilling shapes.

8. MARQUISE

Make a loose coil, press the middle, and glue the end. Hide the glued end by positioning it on one of the pointed ends.

9. MARQUISE WITH SINGLE CURVED END

Make a marquise and bend one of the pinched ends. This shape is commonly used in making leaves.

10. MARQUISE WITH DOUBLE CURVED ENDS

Pinch both ends of a marquise and bend them opposite directions. This shape is also commonly used in making leaves.

11. OFF-CENTER MARQUISE

Make a marquise and pull the center to one side and pinch the opposite end. This shape is used in making flower petals.

12. OVAL

Make a loose coil and press the middle gently to form an oval shape.

13. OFF-CENTER HALF-MOON

Make a loose coil and pull the center toward one corner. Using both hands, form a half-moon shape.

14. CENTERED HALF-MOON

Using both hands, make a loose coil and form a half-moon shape.

15. CRESCENT MOON

Using both hands, make a loose roll and form a crescent shape.

16. ARROWHEAD

Make a loose coil. Pinch one end to make it pointed. Holding the pinched end, use an awl or stick and push in the opposite side to form an arrowhead shape.

17. BUNNY EAR

Make a loose coil. Use an awl or stick to push one edge toward the center to form a bunny ear shape.

18. LILY OF THE VALLEY

Make a bunny ear and bend both ears outward.

19. HEART

Make a loose roll. Use an awl or stick to push one side of the coil toward the center to form a heart shape.

20. HALF CIRCLE

Make a loose coil. Using both hands, form a half circle, .

21. ELONGATED TEARDROP

Make a loose coil and move the center to one corner. After pinching the opposite side of the center tightly, use your fingers to make the entire shape longer.

22. TEARDROP

Make a loose coil and move the center to one corner. Pinch the opposite side.

23. CURVED TEARDROP

Make a teardrop and bend the pointed end.

24. ANGLED MARQUISE

Make a marquise and push one end toward the center, forming angles.

25. SQUARE

Make a marquise. Push the pointed ends toward the center and make four pointed ends.

26. RECTANGLE

Make a marquise. Slightly rotate the shape and push the pointed ends toward the center.

27. TRIANGLE

Make a loose coil. Form a triangular shape, using both hands.

28. HOLLY LEAF

Make a marquise. Pinch six points, then use a stick to curve the sides.

Eccentric Rolls

29. ECCENTRIC LOOSE COIL

Make an evenly spaced loose coil and place it on a quilling board. Using a straight pin, move the center to one side and fix/stick it to the corkboard. Glue the center in place and wait until it dries. When the glue has dried completely, remove the pin carefully.
If the glue is half-dried or the pin still has glue on it, you could ruin the shape.

30. ECCENTRIC TEARDROP

Make an eccentric loose coil. Pinch the opposite end to form a teardrop.

31. ECCENTRIC LONG TEARDROP

Make an eccentric loose coil. Press the entire circle and use your fingers to make the entire shape longer.

32. ECCENTRIC MARQUISE

Make an eccentric loose circle and position the glued center to one side. Pinch both sides of the circle to make two points.

Scrolls

Scrolls are useful for making bushes, snowflakes, border decorations, and geometric designs.

33. LOOSE SCROLL

Make a tight coil. Release and allow it to loosen naturally.

34. CLOSED HEART SCROLL

Fold a strip in half and roll both ends toward the center fold. Release the scrolls and allow them to loosen naturally. Glue the two scrolls together.

35. OPEN HEART SCROLL

Fold a strip in half and roll both ends toward the center fold. Release the scrolls and allow them to loosen naturally.

36. S SCROLL

You can make a natural S-shaped scroll by rolling one end of a strip tightly to the center of a paper strip. Reverse the paper strip and roll the other end to the center. Release the scrolls and allow them to loosen naturally.

37. Uneven S Scroll

Roll two-thirds of a paper strip and release. Reverse the paper strip and roll the remaining one-third tightly to form an uneven S scroll.

38. Musical Note

Fold a strip in half and roll the open ends together toward the folded end to form a musical note.

39. Same-Side Scroll

Fold a strip in half and roll each end toward the center tightly. Release and allow the scrolls to loosen naturally.

40. V Scroll

Fold a strip in half to mark the center. Roll each end from the outward side opposite the fold to make a V-shaped scroll.

41. Uneven V Scroll

Fold a strip so that each side is a different length. Roll each end outward from the fold to form an uneven V-shaped scroll.

42. C Scroll

Roll both ends of a strip inward tightly. Release and allow the scrolls to loosen naturally.

43. Uneven C Scroll

Roll two-thirds of a strip from one end and release. Roll the remaining one-third of the strip and release. You will have an uneven C-shaped scroll.

44. Double Tight Coil

Roll two paper strips together into a tight coil. At the end, the inner strip will be longer. Cut the inner strip shorter than the outer strip. Glue the outer strip.

45. Double Loose Scroll

Roll two paper strips tightly to form a coil. Release and allow the scroll to loosen naturally.

Additional Shapes and Techniques

FRINGED FLOWER

Fringed flowers can be made with a fringing tool or with scissors. A fringing machine can only be used with paper strips that are wider than $3/16$" (4.8 mm). Scissors, however, can be used for all strips $1/8$" (3 mm) and wider. For example, to fringe a $1/4$" (6 mm) -wide strip, place a $1/16$" (1.6 mm) -wide piece of thick paper on one side of the strip and finely cut the remaining $5/32$" (4 mm) with the scissors. Using scissors to make fringes is a painstaking process that requires time and patience. A fringing tool has the advantage of letting you choose various cutting widths according to your needs. Make a tight coil using a fringed paper strip. Hold it with your fingers and spread the fringes with your thumb.

TWO-TONE FRINGED FLOWER

Prepare two different color paper strips of the same width. Cut fringes, using a fringing tool. Make a tight coil with the strips to make a fringed flower.

FRINGED FLOWER WITH A CENTER

Prepare two paper strips of different widths. For example, make a tight coil with a $1/8$" (3 mm) -wide strip, then roll a $1/4$" (6 mm) fringed strip around the tight coil. Spread the fringes.

LOOP HUSKING AND FAN HUSKING

In order to make loop and fan huskings, you need a quilling corkboard, straight pins, graph paper, and transparent plastic paper. Place a sheet of graph paper and transparent plastic paper on top of the corkboard. Place the pins according to your design. Wrap a paper strip around the pins and glue as seen in Figures 1 and 2. This a good technique for making multiple uniform shapes; however, it is a delicate process as you have to frequently reposition the pins. Here is how to make a vertical loop husking: First, make a long loop and hold it with one hand. Continue making three or four loops, keeping the loops equidistant from one another (Figure 3.1). A fan husking can be created by making a long loop in the center, then continue making loops alternately on the right and left sides, as shown in Figures 3.2 and 3.3. Finally, wrap all the loops together once or twice. You can make the husking unique by winding two paper strips together.

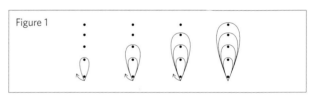

Figure 1

Figure 2

Figure 3

3.1 Four-Loop Vertical Husking
3.2 Five-Loop Fan Husking
3.3 Seven-Loop Fan Husking

Bell Shape and Grape Roll

Make a tight coil and push out the center to form a cone shape. Lightly hold the roll with your thumb and index finger, and rub it to form a bell shape. During this process, you have to be very careful not to use too much force, as the center of the coil might slip out. Apply glue to the inside to maintain its shape. Bells can be used as planting pots or as the body and limbs of a small doll. To make grape rolls, make a tight coil and push out the center slightly. Apply glue to the inside of the shape and allow it to dry.

Spirals

Place one end of a paper strip on your index finger and position a quilling needle tool at a 45-degree angle. Hold the paper strip between your thumb and index finger on the hand holding the needle tool and, with the other hand, lightly press and roll the strip. This will naturally form a spiral shape. Spirals are useful for making flower stems and ivy. Using four or five spirals together is especially useful when making flower wreaths. (See Spiral Christmas Wreath with Bells, page 83.)

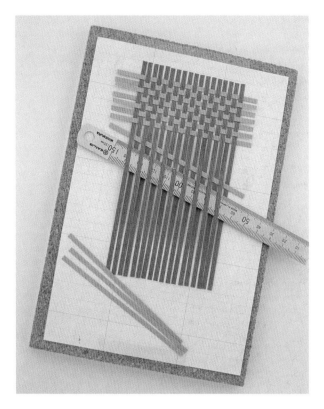

Weaving Paper Strips

Use clear plastic tape to affix a sheet of graph paper to the quilling corkboard. Put the required length of double-sided tape across the top of a piece of graph paper. Stick paper strips vertically across the top of the paper, taking care to keep them parallel. If you place the paper strips too tightly, it will be hard to insert the horizontal strips. If you place them too loosely, you will end up with a lot of empty spaces. You can make the process easier by using a metal ruler to lift alternating paper strips. When using $1/8$" (3 mm) strips, it is appropriate to have less than $1/16$" (1.6 mm) spacing. This technique is also useful for making baskets or backgrounds.

Figure 1

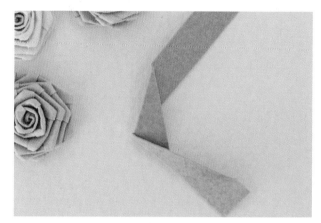

Figure 2

Figure 3

Figure 4

HOW TO MAKE A FOLDED ROSE

You can make roses using $5/16$" (8 mm) -wide (or wider) paper strips. Fold one end of a strip twice diagonally at 15 degrees (Figure 1). Fold the longer end back to the folded angled point so that it forms a 130-degree angle (Figure 2). Take the angled end that was created when you made the first two folds, and roll it until you meet another angled end. Then fold the strip back again to form another 130-degree angle (Figure 3). Repeat the folding process until you reach the end of the paper strip. Glue the end and you will have a folded rose shape (Figure 4).

FLOWERS MADE USING PAPER CUTOUTS

Cut eighteen equal-size flower petals, using a template. Fringe the petals by making alternately short and long cuts in the petal edge toward the bottom end of the petal. Slightly fold the bottom end of the petal back. Slightly curve the top part of each petal, using an awl. Cut out a $5/8$" (1.6 cm) -diameter paper circle. Using tweezers, glue six petals to the circle to form the base of the flower. Glue six more petals on top of the base petals. Glue four more petals to the center. Cut the remaining two petals in half and glue these to fill the remaining space. Make a fringed flower with a $3/16$" (4.8 mm) -wide strip and glue it to the center of the flower. (See A Blue Cornflower and Daisy Arrangement, page 49.)

Quilling Tips and Techniques

By making good use of these tips, you will save time and simplify your work process. Additionally, you will also gain more confidence as you use these techniques repeatedly.

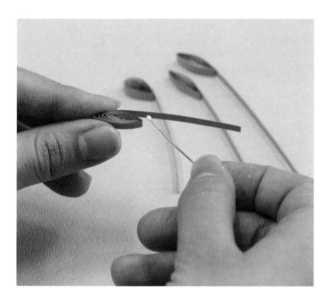

STEMS WITH LEAVES

Usually, stems and leaves are made separately and then glued together. However, if you make them using a single process, that is a real time saver. First, prepare paper strips calculating the length needed to roll the leaf and the length of the stem together. For example, if the length needed to roll a leaf is one-third of one paper strip, add the desired stem length and prepare a longer strip. When the paper strip is ready, roll the marquise or teardrop and glue it, leaving the remainder of the strip unrolled.

ORGANIZING TIPS FOR PAPER STRIPS

Paper strip lengths vary among brands. In some cases, it is necessary to bend longer strips several times to store them in plastic or resealable bags. However, paper strips used in this book are relatively short, 10 ⁵⁄₈" (27 cm) and, therefore, are very easy to store. Separate your paper strips by color and store them in plastic bags, drawers, or plastic boxes.

HOW TO USE GLUE

There are various types of glue. In the past, most containers had wide openings, and the glue had to be scooped out and used immediately to avoid drying out. But these days, there are containers specially designed for paper quilling. Here is a way to use glue without having to constantly open and close the lid: Prepare a container that is slightly larger than the container of glue and place a wet paper tissue in the bottom. Place the container of glue with the top open, upside down in the larger container. The wet tissue will prevent the opening from drying out while you are working on your project.

STORING FINISHED PIECES

There are occasions when pieces such as flowers or leaves become unusable due to lack of care; creased or crushed pieces cannot be repaired; contact with air and light can make papers brittle or change their colors. Always follow proper storage methods right from the start. It is always recommended to use small, airtight boxes or plastic containers to store pieces. Or, you can put them in resealable plastic bags first and then store them in boxes.

HOW TO USE TOOLS

When rolling paper strips, you must use a quilling needle tool or tweezers; then, when the shape is formed, you will have to pick up a straight pin to apply a tiny drop of glue. This is quite troublesome. You can save time and simplify the process by placing a pin between two fingers while you are using the tweezers to roll the strips. Then the pin is available whenever it is needed. This technique will take practive at first, but eventually you will become accustomed to it.

COLLECTING IDEAS

To make your own original pieces, look for inspiration by reading magazines, studying quilling pattern books, and visiting exhibitions or bookstores. It is important to draw sketches or make notes whenever you think of new ideas.

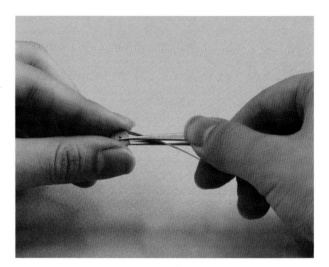

ROLLING PAPER STRIPS WITH TWEEZERS

It is not easy to roll thin paper strips, but you can make it easier by using tweezers instead of your fingers. At first, this technique may seem difficult, but eventually you will become accustomed to it through practice.

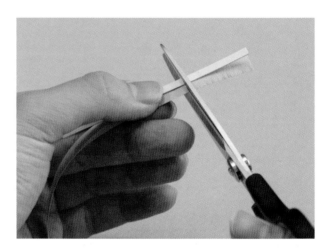

USING A THICK PIECE OF PAPER WHEN MAKING FRINGED FLOWERS WITH SCISSORS

It is very convenient to make fringed flowers using a fringing tool. However, you can use scissors to make fringed flowers when a fringing tool is unavailable or when you need to fringe $1/8$" (3 mm) -wide strips. For example, when fringing

¼" (6 mm) strips, place a ¹⁄₁₆" (1.6 mm) -wide piece of thick paper on one side of the paper strip to the depth of the desired fringe, then lightly cut the edge with scissors. Finely cut the remaining ⁵⁄₃₂" (4 mm), using scissors. This will minimize the number of broken or torn strips.

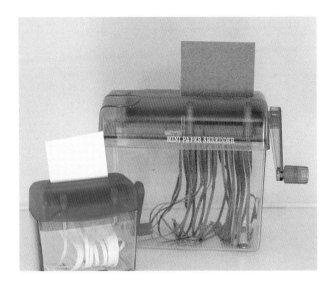

HOW TO MAKE PAPER STRIPS USING A MINI PAPER SHREDDER

Generally, paper strips are purchased through stores, but you can cut your own paper strips to suit your artwork. In this case, a mini paper shredder can be a good substitute for scissors. When using a shredder, the edges of the strips may be rough, however, this may allow you to create unique soft textures. You can also make strips in any color or length you desire.

STREAMLINING PRODUCTION

When working on a complicated project, there are occasions when you have to repeatedly make the same shapes. You can save time by rolling all the required shapes first, then assembling the flowers or leaves, rather than assembling individual flowers and leaves as you go.

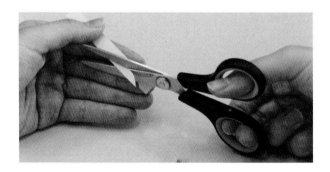

WORKING ON A PIECE OF PLASTIC OR A CD

If you use a small piece of plastic or a recycled CD when gluing pieces, it is easy to remove them when they are dry. Plastic and CDs also allow you to rotate the pieces, making the work much easier to manipulate.

HOW TO CUT LEAVES

Make a lengthwise crease in the middle of a paper strip and fold. If you are not used to cutting leaf shapes, you may draw them and cut them out, but after practicing a few times you will be able to cut them freehand. To make a modified leaf shape, make diagonal cuts in the edges of the folded leaves.

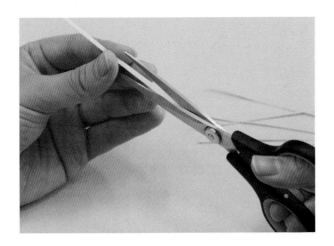

Cutting Paper Strips in Half Lengthwise

It is appropriate to use narrow $\frac{1}{16}$" (1.6 mm) -wide paper strips for the centers of small flowers. For example, when making teardrop or marquise flowers with quarter-length paper strips, if you used $\frac{1}{8}$" (3 mm) -wide strips for the center, the proportion would be strange as this is the same width as the flower. Instead, cut $\frac{1}{8}$" (3 mm) strips in half lengthwise to make the centers for small flowers. This is an important part of the greeting cards and name cards (see page 53) in this book that are made with small flowers.

How to Create a Three-Dimensional Look

You can create a three-dimensional look by gluing flowers in bunches, rather than gluing them one by one, to a flat surface. You can assemble flowers quickly by applying a sufficient amount of glue and allowing them to dry completely. Another method that does not require glue is to use thick double-sided tape applied to the back of flowers.

Before You Start

1. All art work in this book is made using $\frac{1}{8}$" (3 mm) -wide paper strips, unless otherwise indicated.

2. Although the colors used in these projects are listed for your convenience, substitute colors can be used to suit your taste. You can also create your own original work by modifying these designs with your own ideas.

3. Paper quilling is a process that requires repeatedly making the same size shapes and flowers. Because these shapes are made by hand, each one will be different. So, you should focus on the overall look of the artwork.

For Reference

Quilling needle thickness: $\frac{1}{32}$" (0.8 mm)
Awl thickness: $\frac{1}{16}$" (1.6 mm)
Bamboo thickness: $\frac{1}{8}$", $\frac{5}{32}$", and $\frac{3}{16}$" (3 mm, 4 mm, and 4.8 mm)

Whispering Flowers
Size: 15 ¾" × 21 ⅝" (40 × 55 cm)

Paper Quilling
Projects

Paper Quilling Designs for Framing

Greeting Cards

Decorative Frame Borders and Plaques

Christmas Wreaths and Snowflakes

Paper Picture Frames and Gift Boxes

Here is a collection of beautiful and practical paper-quilling projects. By working on these projects you will eventually be able to branch out and create your very own designs. Use colorful paper strips to make items such as photo frames, cards, wall hangings, or potpourri sachets. These will be great gifts for someone very special.

Paper Quilling Designs for Framing

The projects in this section will yield beautiful frameable pieces for enliving the décor of any room in your home. Given as gifts, they will recall the small flowers of early spring, newly blossoming violets, or, perhaps, a birthday bouquet given long ago that is now a lasting reminder of that special time. From simple designs for beginners to complicated designs that require some experience, these projects will expose you to limitless possibilities of paper quilling.

Note: All projects in this book use ⅛" (3 mm) -wide paper strips, unless the width and length are indicated otherwise. Also, for convenience, 10⅝" (27 cm) -long paper strips are divided into ½ (5⅜" [13.5 cm]), ⅓ (3½" [9 cm]), ¼ (2¹¹⁄₁₆" [6.8 cm]), and ⅛ (1⁵⁄₁₆" [3.4 cm]) lengths. (See page 12)

Yellow Wildflower

A good project for beginners, this project is made with marquises. It is suitable for greeting cards or small frames.

Size: 4¾" × 4¾" (12 × 12 cm)

Yellow Marquise Flower in Full Bloom

Make a flower with eight marquises, using ½-length canary yellow strips. Make a tight coil, using a ⅓-length orange strip and glue it to the center of the flower.

Yellow Marquise Flower with Three or Four Petals

Make seven marquises, using ½-length canary yellow strips. Use the marquises to make one flower with three petals and one flower with four petals. Make bunny ears, using ⅓-length olive green strips. Use the bunny ears as flower cups.

Leaves and Stems

Make thirteen marquises, using ⅓-length olive green strips. Make five more marquises, using ¼-length olive strips. Prepare one 1⅜" (3.5 cm) -long and two 2½" (6.5 cm) -long moss green strips.

Stems with Leaves

Make ten marquises, using ⅓- and ¼-length olive green strips. Use ¾" (1.9 cm) -long moss green strips for stems. Make two stems with leaves: one with seven marquises and another with three marquises.

Stems

Prepare one 1⅜" (3.5 cm) -long and two 2½" (6.4 cm) -long moss green strips.

Assembly

1. Glue the yellow marquise flower in full bloom, the three-petal yellow marquise, and the four-petal yellow marquise flowers in place.

2. Glue the stems to the flowers, and glue the stems with leaves and the marquise-shaped leaves in place.

Actual size

English Garden Flowers

These flowers are made from various basic shapes and with one look you can see the variety of paper quilling techniques being used. This colorful project is ideal for beginners and will teach basic paper quilling shapes and techniques.

Size: 6¾" × 6" (17 × 15 cm)

YELLOW MARQUISE FLOWER

Make a flower with eight ovals, using ½-length yellow strips. Make a tight coil, using a ⅓-length white strip. Glue the coil to the center of the flower.

LEAVES AND STEM FOR YELLOW FLOWER

Layer one olive green and one khaki strip together. Fold the strips in a zigzag pattern as seen in Figure 1. Press the pattern together and apply glue to the inside of the leaf. Make four leaves as seen in Figure 2. Glue the leaves to a 3" (7.5 cm) -long moss green strip.

1   2

Orange Marquise Flower

For a flower center, make a marquise, using a $\frac{1}{3}$-length dusty yellow strip. Make seven off-center marquises, using $\frac{1}{2}$-length orange strips. Place the orange marquises below the flower center and glue them tightly together. To make stamens, use five $\frac{1}{32}$" (0.8 mm) -wide and $\frac{3}{8}$" (1 cm) -long yellow strips. Roll the ends to the center of the strips. Glue the stamens above the flower's center.

Leaves and Stem for Orange Flower

Make three marquises, using $\frac{2}{5}$-length moss green strips. Make three more, using $\frac{1}{2}$-length moss green strips. Alternately glue the leaves to a $2\frac{3}{4}$" (7 cm) -long olive green stem.

Purple Teardrop Flower

Make a teardrop, using a full-length purple strip. Wrap a light purple strip around it twice. Glue five petals together to form the flower. Make a tight coil, using a $\frac{1}{3}$-length canary yellow strip, and glue the coil to the center of the flower.

Leaves and Stem for Purple Flower

Make four off-center marquises, using $\frac{2}{5}$-length olive green strips. Make four more, using $\frac{1}{2}$-length olive green strips. Attach the leaves in pairs on opposite sides of a slightly curved $3\frac{1}{4}$" (8.2 cm) -long khaki stem.

Pink Bunny Ear Flower

Using $\frac{1}{2}$-length strips, make three pink and three light pink bunny ears. Make a tight coil, using a $\frac{1}{3}$-length kiwi strip, and glue it to the center of the flower.

Leaves and Stem for Pink Flower

Make six big leaves and two small leaves from moss green three-loop vertical huskings. Alternately glue the leaves to a 3" (7.5 cm) -long khaki stem.

Lavender Teardrop Flower

Make six teardrops, using $\frac{1}{2}$-length lavender strips, and glue them together. Make a tight coil, using a $\frac{1}{4}$-length orange strip, and glue it to the center of the flower.

Leaves and Stem for Lavender Flower

Make three leaves. For each leaf, roll three marquises, using $\frac{1}{3}$-length khaki strips. Make two more leaves. For each leaf, roll three marquises from $\frac{1}{3}$-length olive green strips. Alternately glue the leaves to a $2\frac{1}{2}$" (6.5 cm) -long olive green stem.

Assembly

1. Glue the purple flower in the center.

2. Glue the pink and lavender flowers on the right side and the orange and yellow flowers on the left.

80% of actual size

Violet Bouquet

To make the flowers stand out, this project uses teardrop flowers wrapped with strips of the same bright color family. The rich yellow ribbon and purple flower combination especially brings out the essence of paper quilling. This project can be used to make greeting cards, or it can be applied to small frames.

Size: 4" × 4" (10 × 10 cm)

Purple Teardrop Flowers

Make fifteen teardrops, using $\frac{1}{2}$-length purple strips. Wrap each teardrop once with bright blue. Make three flowers, using five teardrops for each. Make a tight coil, using a $\frac{1}{3}$-length yellow strip, and glue the coil to the center of flower.

Light Purple Marquise Flower

Make five flowers. For each flower, make three marquises, using $\frac{1}{4}$-length light purple strips.

Flower Cup and Leaves

Prepare two 1" (2.5 cm) -long moss green strips. Glue the two strips together, leaving $\frac{5}{8}$" (1.6 cm) unglued. Cut the unglued ends to make them pointy. Make five flower cups by slightly curving the pointy ends. Glue the light purple flowers to the flower cups. Make teardrops, using $\frac{1}{4}$-length olive green strips. Glue two teardrops to each stem.

Leaves

Make four leaves with three teardrops each; one teardrop from a $\frac{1}{3}$-length olive green strip and two teardrops from $\frac{1}{3}$-length sage green strips. Make an additional two teardrops, using $\frac{1}{3}$-length sage green strips.

Ribbon

Make two bunny ears and two arrowheads, using full-length canary yellow strips. Glue these together as shown in the picture.

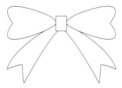

Stems

Make stems, using nine slightly curved 1" (2.5 cm) -long sage green strips.

Pollen

Stick a bright blue paper strip to one side of a piece of double-sided tape. Cut eight small triangles.

Assembly

1. Glue the three purple teardrop flowers in the center.

2. Glue the light purple flowers around the purple teardrop flowers proportionally.

3. Glue the leaves in the spaces between the light purple flowers.

4. Glue the nine stems below the purple teardrop flowers and attach the ribbon just above them.

5. Decorate the empty spaces with the pollen shapes.

Actual size

A Basket of Flowers

This is a very useful project for learning how to weave a basket pattern. Various types of baskets and textures can be created by using different width paper strips and colors. In this project, a three-dimensional look is created by using marquises, fringed flowers, and teardrops.

Size: 5⅛" × 6¼" (13 × 16 cm)

Pastel Green Marquise Flowers

Make eight flowers. For each one, make six marquises, using $1/3$-length pastel green strips. Make tight coils, using $1/4$- and $1/6$-length yellow strips. Use the coils for flower centers.

Tangerine Teardrop Flower

Make four flowers. For each flower, make five teardrops, using $1/4$-length tangerine strips. Make tight coils, using $1/6$-length strips. Use the coils for flower centers.

Fringed Flowers

Make five fringed flowers, using $2\,1/3$" × 6" (6 × 15 cm) paper strips.

Stem with Leaves

Make forty to fifty marquises, each with a single curved end. Glue five to seven of them to each 2" (5 cm) -long stem. Make a total of seven stems with leaves.

1$1/2$" (3.8 cm)

1$7/8$" (4.8 cm)
Actual size

1$1/4$" (3 cm)

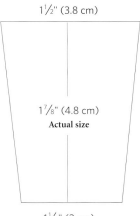

1

2

3

85% of actual size

Basket

Prepare eight $3/16$" (5 mm) -wide by $4\,1/2$" (11.5 cm) -long white strips and twenty-five $1/8$" (3 mm) -wide by $2\,7/8$" (7.2 cm) -long white strips. Glue eight of the $3/16$" (5 mm) -wide strips vertically every $1/16$" (1.6 mm) across. Start weaving by alternately inserting the $1/8$" (3 mm) -wide strips (see Figure 1). When the woven piece reaches $2\,3/8$" × 3" (6 × 7.5 cm), apply glue on top of it and allow it to dry. Cut a basket shape from a thick piece of paper, using a template, and glue it to the woven piece. Trim the woven piece leaving a margin for folding (see Figure 2). Fold the margin back so that it has the shape of a basket and glue it (see Figure 3). Make two spirals, using $1/16$" (1.6 mm) -wide by $3\,3/16$" (8 cm) -long white strips. Glue the spirals to the top and bottom of the basket.

Assembly

1. Glue the basket in the lower center.

2. Glue six pastel green flowers, (opposite page). Glue the seven stems with leaves.

3. Glue the four fringed flowers in the remaining spaces. Place one fringed flower on top of a pastel green flower.

4. Glue four tangerine flowers and two pastel green flowers on top of the other flowers for a three-dimensional look.

Wildflower Bouquet

This project, with small flowers gathered in harmony, could be quite challenging for a beginner. However, by practicing these techniques, you can learn to make beautiful greeting cards and small frameable decorations. If making small flowers is too difficult, increase the paper strip lengths to make the flowers twice the size.

Size: 3½" × 5" (9 × 13 cm)

BRIGHT BLUE BUNNY EAR FLOWER

Make three flowers. For each flower, make five bunny ears, using ½-length bright blue strips. Make tight coils, using ⅓-length white strips. Use the coils as flower centers.

BLUE MARQUISE FLOWER

Make nine flowers. For each flower, use a ⅛" (3 mm) -thick bamboo stick to make five tight coils with a center hole, using ⅛-length blue strips. Then roll a tight coil, using a ¹⁄₁₆" (1.6 mm) -wide by ¹⁄₁₆-length canary yellow strip, and glue it to the center of the flower.

YELLOW TEARDROP FLOWER

Make four flowers. For each flower, use a needle tool to make four tight coils with a center hole, using ⅛-length yellow strips. Glue four coils together to form one flower.

LARGE LEAVES

Make two marquises with single curved end, using a ½-length olive green strips, and three more, using ½-length moss green strips.

SMALL LEAVES

Make a marquise with single curved end, using a ¼-length olive green strip, and one more, using a ¼-length moss green strip.

RIBBON

Prepare one ¼" (6 mm) -wide by 2⅛" (5.4 cm) -long (upper ribbon layer) and one ¼" (6 mm) -wide by 2⅜" (6 cm) -long (bottom ribbon layer) grass green paper strip. Fold both in half to mark the center of the strips. Fold the ends toward the center and glue them. Glue the upper

5.5 cm

6 cm

8 cm

layer and lower layer together, and wrap the center with a ⁵⁄₁₆" (8 mm) -wide full-length bright green strip. Prepare a ¼" (6 mm) -wide by 3¼" (8.2 cm) -long bright green paper strip. Make a small cut in the center to allow the ends to bend downward. Cut a V shape into both ends of the ribbon. Glue it to the center of the ribbon.

STEMS

Make four spirals with 2¼" (5.7 cm) -long light green paper strips. Cut each to 1⅝" (4 cm) long.

ASSEMBLY

1. Glue three bright blue bunny ear flowers in the center. Glue nine small blue marquise flowers above them.

2. Glue three yellow teardrop flowers on the left side and one on the right side.

3. Glue the large and small leaves in the empty spaces.

4. Glue the spiral stems below the bright blue bunny ear flowers. Add the ribbon on top of the stems.

90% of actual size

Flowers in Spring

This project uses petals made from three or four elements and has a delicate and lifelike quality. It has a high level of difficulty and requires quilling experience. The leaves are also made with several marquises bunched and glued together.

Size: 6" × 8¹⁄₄" (15 × 21 cm)

YELLOW FLOWERS

Make twenty-four flowers. For each flower, make five tight coils with a center hole, using $1/8$-length yellow strips.

STEMS

Prepare five 5" (12.7 cm) -long moss green strips. Glue them together, leaving $3/8$" (1 cm) from the end unglued. Spread the unglued ends. Glue five yellow flowers above the spread ends, and glue six more yellow flowers above those. Repeat to make a total of two stems.

PURPLE FLOWERS

Make angled marquises with full-length purple strips. Wrap a moss green strip twice around each. Make three three-petal flowers.

STEMS

Glue five 4" (10 cm) -long moss green strips together and bend the upper portion. Make a wide or narrow bend in the stems according to the desired position of the purple flower.

YELLOW FLOWER WRAPPED IN WHITE STRIPS

Make two half-moon shapes. Fold a $5/16$" (8 mm) -long tangerine strip in half and connect a $1/2$-length yellow strip, then make a four-loop vertical husking. To form the petal, position the loops between two half-moons. Wrap the finished petal with a full-length white strip, leaving some space at the tips of the petals.

60% of actual size

FLOWER CENTER

After making three tight coils, using $1/8$-length yellow strips, wrap them three times with a light green strip.

STEMS

Make stems by gluing five $2\,1/8$" (5.4 cm) -long strips together.

LEAVES

Roll about ninety marquises with double curved ends, using $1/2$-length moss green and sage green strips. Connect eight of the marquises together to form a row, then do the same for another seven. Glue the two rows of leaves together. Before the glue dries completely, use your hands to form a leaf shape. Wrap the leaf with a moss green strip.

ASSEMBLY

1. Position one yellow flower in the upper center and the other slightly lower.

2. Glue leaves to the right and left of the yellow flowers. Glue the purple flowers, placing the stems in between the leaves.

3. Place the yellow flower wrapped in white strips on top of the purple flower. Add the stems and leaves.

Flowers in the Garden

This dazzling and whimsical beauty of the garden is created with two-tone and white off-center teardrop flowers. By working on this project, you can master off-center shapes, using a quilling corkboard.

Size: 6" × 6" (15 × 15 cm)

PURPLE AND LAVENDER FLOWERS IN FULL BLOOM

Make five flowers. For each flower, roll two lavender and three purple angled marquises, using full-length paper strips for each. Make tight coils with $\frac{1}{4}$-length canary yellow strips, for the flower centers.

FLOWER BUD IN PURPLE AND LAVENDER

Make petals, using the same method as above. Make a grape roll, using a $\frac{1}{2}$-length kiwi strip. Use the grape roll as a flower cup.

WHITE IRREGULAR TEARDROP FLOWER

Make three flowers. For each flower, make five irregular teardrops, using $\frac{2}{3}$-length white strips. Then roll three tight coils, using $\frac{1}{8}$-length yellow strips, wrap each twice with canary yellow, and glue to the center of the flower.

STEMS WITH LEAVES

Make about forty bunny ears with $\frac{1}{8}$-, $\frac{1}{7}$-, and $\frac{1}{6}$-length light blue strips. Glue them to $3\frac{1}{8}$" (8 cm) -long stems according to size. Add a tight coil to the tip of each stem.

LEAVES

Make seven leaves. For each one, make five marquises, using $\frac{1}{3}$-length moss green strips.

POLLEN

Stick a yellow paper strip to a piece of double-sided tape. Cut about ten small triangle pieces.

ASSEMBLY

1. Glue three stems with leaves in the center of the background.

2. Stick double-sided tape to the five purple and lavender flowers in full bloom and the white irregular teardrop flowers. Glue them in the center.

3. Glue the leaves between the flowers and add the yellow pollen for decoration.

90% of actual size

A Blue Cornflower and Daisy Arrangement

Blue flowers made with cut-out paper are very three-dimensional and colorful. The white paper strips used in this project are cut with a paper shredder and wrapped with canary yellow strips. This technique gives the artwork a unique texture and a lifelike quality.

Size: 9⁷⁄₈" × 7⁷⁄₈" (25 × 20 cm)

1   2   3   4   5

LARGE AND SMALL FLOWERS MADE WITH CUT-OUT PAPER

Copy or draw the template onto bright blue paper (Figure 1).
Cut out eighteen petals. Fringe the edges of the petals
(Figure 2). Slightly fold the bottom end of the petal back.
Slightly curve the top part of each petal, using an awl. Using
tweezers, glue six petals to a small circle (Figure 3). Glue six
more petals on top of them to form the center of the flower
(Figure 4). Glue four more petals to the center. Cut the
remaining two petals in half and glue them between the
petals (Figure 5). Make fringed
flowers with $1/4$" (6 mm) -wide by
$7\,7/8$" (20 cm) -long canary yellow
paper strips, and glue one to the
center of each flower.

WHITE FLOWERS WRAPPED IN YELLOW AND A SMALL FLOWER

Make seven teardrops, using full-length
white strips. Wrap each teardrop twice
with a canary yellow strip. Make twelve large flowers with
seven petals each. Make one small white flower, using $3/4$-
length strips. Roll tight coils, using $1/2$-length tangerine and
canary strips. Glue the coils to the flower centers. (The
white flowers will have more texture, as they were cut
with a paper shredder).

DARK GREEN LEAVES

Make fourteen leaves. For each leaf, make six or eight
marquises with single curved end, using $1/3$-length dark
green strips.

LEAVES WRAPPED WITH OLIVE GREEN

Roll fifty-five marquises, using full-length yellow-green strips.
Wrap each once with olive green. Make eleven leaves with
five marquises each.

ASSEMBLY

1. Glue the one large and two small flowers made
with cut-out paper in the center.

2. Glue six white flowers wrapped in yellow around the
cut-out paper blue flowers. Position the leaves appro-
priately while considering the overall appearance.

3. Position the remaining white flowers beneath the
blue flowers or on top of the leaves for a three-
dimensional look.

60% of actual size

Red Floral Bouquet

In this project, exuberant red flowers and small blue flowers are mixed in a colorful harmony. Here, you will learn to make two-color ribbons and flowers using various types of rolls.

Size: 6" × 7⅞" (15 × 20 cm)

Bright Red Marquise Flowers in Full Bloom

Make two large flowers. For each flower, make nine marquises, using full-length bright red strips. Make another smaller flower with eight marquises. Make tight coils and form grape rolls, using full-length canary yellow strips. Glue the grape rolls to the flower centers.

Flower Buds

Make two flower buds. For each one, make three marquises, using bright red full-length strips. Make bell shapes with $\frac{1}{2}$-length olive green strips for the flower cups.

Orange Flowers Made with Two Shapes

Make two off-center half-moons with $\frac{1}{2}$-length orange strips. Make a four-loop vertical husking, using a $\frac{1}{3}$-length

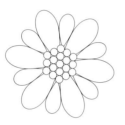

orange strip. Place the husking in the center and glue the off-center half-moons on each side. Wrap an orange strip twice around the combined pieces and glue. Make two flowers with six petals each. To complete each flower, roll six teardrops with $\frac{1}{2}$-length bright red strips and insert them between the orange petals. Roll seven tight coils with a needle tool, using $\frac{1}{8}$-length tangerine strips. Glue the coils to the center of the flower. Make twelve tight coils, using $\frac{1}{8}$-length black strips and glue them around the tangerine coils.

Turquoise, Sky Blue, and Dark Blue Teardrop Flowers

Make eight flowers. For each flower, make five teardrops, using $\frac{1}{3}$-length turquoise, sky blue, or dark blue strips. Roll tight coils, using $\frac{1}{6}$-length light sky blue, canary yellow, and tangerine strips. Glue the coils to the flower centers.

Leaves

Make two leaves. For each leaf, roll three marquises, using $\frac{1}{2}$-length olive green strips.

Stems with Leaves

Prepare olive green strips $1\frac{1}{4}$" (3 cm) or $1\frac{5}{8}$" (4 cm) longer than a $\frac{1}{3}$-length strip. Roll only the $\frac{1}{3}$-length into a marquise. Use the remaining length as a stem. Make several marquises, using $\frac{1}{3}$-length olive green and moss green strips. Glue two or three marquises to each stem.

Ribbon

Mark the center on a $\frac{3}{8}$" (1 cm) -wide by $4\frac{3}{8}$" (11 cm) -long (upper layer) and a $\frac{3}{8}$" (1 cm) -wide by $4\frac{3}{4}$" (12 cm) -long (bottom layer) light purple strip. Fold and glue the ends to meet in the center. Glue a $\frac{1}{8}$" (3 mm) -wide by $4\frac{3}{8}$" (11 cm) -long and a $\frac{1}{8}$" (3 mm) -wide by $4\frac{3}{8}$" (11 cm) -long pastel purple strip along the middle of the light purple strips. Glue the two ribbon layers together. Wrap the center vertically, using a $\frac{1}{4}$" (6 mm) -wide by $\frac{3}{8}$" (1 cm) -long strip. Add two $1\frac{5}{8}$" (4 cm) -long ribbons as streamers.

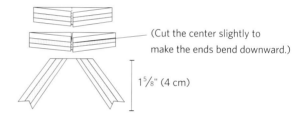

(Cut the center slightly to make the ends bend downward.)

$1\frac{5}{8}$" (4 cm)

Flower Stems

Using a needle tool, make spirals, using 2" (5.1 cm), $2\frac{1}{4}$" (5.7 cm), and $2\frac{1}{2}$" (6.4 cm) -long forest green and grass green strips.

Assembly

1. Glue two large bright red flowers and the two orange flowers made with two shapes in the center.

2. Glue the small bright red flower above the flowers in the center and add the flower buds.

3. Place the stems with leaves between the flowers. Fill the empty spaces with the blue flowers.

4. Glue the spirals below the flowers and add the ribbon.

See pattern on page 112.

Greeting Cards

Expressing heartfelt gratitude or making an unexpected marriage proposal—all of these sentiments and more can be hidden inside one small card using the techniques described in this section. Send cards designed with lavender teardrop flowers and your loved ones will cherish the quilled card you designed just for them.

Valentine's Day

Size: 5" × 5" (12.5 × 12.5 cm)

PINK AND LIGHT PURPLE BUNNY EAR FLOWERS

Make four pink and four light purple bunny ear flowers, using ¼-length strips.

STEMS WITH LEAVES

Prepare yellow-green strips ½" (1.3 cm) longer than a ¼-length strip. Roll marquises using the ¼-length only. Glue each marquise and use the remaining length as the stem. Make eight marquises using ¼-length yellow-green strips. Glue one marquise to each stem.

VINES

Make eight V scrolls, using ⅙-length white strips.

YELLOW MARQUISE FLOWER BUDS

Make eight marquises, using ⅛-length yellow strips.

HEART

Make a ⅝" (1.6 cm) -diameter circle by winding a yellow strip twice. To make a heart shape, pinch one end of the circle to make a pointed end and push the opposite ends inward, using a needle tool. Make five loose scrolls, using ¾" (1.9 cm) -long yellow and canary yellow strips, and use them to fill the inside of the heart.

ASSEMBLY

1. Glue eight stems with leaves to form a 2¼" (6 cm) -diameter circle.

2. Glue the vines and yellow marquise flower buds.

3. Glue the pink and light purple bunny ear flowers between the leaves, and add the heart to the center of the wreath.

Note: Use tweezers for creating the small shapes in this project.

SEE PATTERN ON PAGE 113.

Happy Birthday I

Size: 5" × 5" (12.5 × 12.5 cm)

RIBBON

Make two bunny ears and two arrowheads, using full-length grape purple strips. Wrap the center of the ribbon with a $\frac{1}{8}$" (3 mm) -wide strip.

LAVENDER MARQUISE FLOWER AND FLOWER BUDS

Make four flowers. For each flower, roll three marquises, using $\frac{1}{6}$-length lavender strips. Make six more marquises for buds.

LAVENDER TIGHT-COIL FLOWER BUDS

Make four tight coils, using $\frac{1}{8}$-length lavender strips.

LEAVES

Make fourteen large and six small leaves. For each leaf, make a three-loop vertical husking, using moss green strips. Make four more leaves. For each leaf, make a two-loop vertical husking.

VINES

Make six loose scrolls with $\frac{1}{6}$-length yellow-green strips, and two more with $\frac{1}{8}$-length yellow-green strips.

POLLEN

Make six tight coils, using $\frac{1}{16}$-length canary yellow strips.

HEART-SHAPED STEM

Fold one $8\frac{1}{4}$" (21 cm) -long moss green strip in half and curve the ends inward. Glue the ends together to form a heart shape.

ASSEMBLY

1. Glue the heart-shaped stem in the center of the card.

2. Glue the large leaves outside the bottom of the heart-shaped stem and glue the small leaves above them.

3. Glue the lavender marquise flowers outside the heart stem and between the leaves. Glue the vines on the inside of the heart shape.

4. Glue the pollen between the flowers and leaves. Add the ribbon in the center of the heart shape.

5. Add "Happy Birthday" to the center of the card.

SEE PATTERN ON PAGE 113.

Wishes and Love

Size: 5" × 5" (12.5 × 12.5 cm)

WHITE MARQUISE FLOWERS

Make four flowers. For each flower, make seven marquises, using $\frac{1}{4}$-length white strips. Then roll a tight coil, using a $\frac{1}{16}$" (1.6 mm) -wide $\frac{1}{8}$-length canary yellow strip, and glue it to the center of the flower.

TURQUOISE BUNNY EAR FLOWERS

Make four flowers. For each flower, make four bunny ears, using $\frac{1}{3}$-length turquoise strips. Then roll a tight coil, using a $\frac{3}{4}$" (1.9 cm) -long yellow strip, and glue it inside the flower center.

STEMS WITH LEAVES

Prepare kiwi paper strips $\frac{3}{8}$" (1 cm) longer than a $\frac{1}{6}$-length strip. Roll marquises, using the $\frac{1}{6}$-length only. Glue the marquise, and use the remaining $\frac{3}{8}$" (1 cm) as the stem. Make marquises, using $\frac{1}{6}$-length kiwi strips, and glue one to each stem. Make four stems with leaves.

VINES AND LEAVES

Make vines, using $\frac{1}{6}$-length kiwi strips. Make marquises, using $\frac{1}{6}$-length kiwi strips, and glue them to the vines.

PASTEL PURPLE TIGHT COILS

Make eight tight coils, using $\frac{1}{8}$-length pastel purple strips.

RIBBON

Make a ribbon, using a $\frac{1}{4}$" (6 mm) -wide by $2\frac{1}{2}$" (6.4 cm) -long pastel purple strip, as shown in the picture.

POLLEN

Stick lavender strips to a piece of double-sided tape and cut eighteen triangles.

ASSEMBLY

1. Glue the white marquise flowers to form a $2\frac{1}{8}$" (5.4 cm) -diameter circle. Add the turquoise flowers between the white flowers.

2. Glue the vines and leaves between the white and turquoise flowers.

3. Glue the pastel purple tight coils between the leaves. Add the ribbon in the center of the wreath.

4. Glue nine lavender pollen pieces above and below the wreath.

SEE PATTERN ON PAGE 113.

The Art of Paper Quilling

Memories of Spring

Size: 5" × 5" (12.5 × 12.5 cm)

Canary Yellow Teardrop Flowers

Make eight elongated teardrops, using $\frac{1}{6}$-length canary yellow strips. Glue $\frac{3}{8}$" (1 cm) -long light green strips to make stems.

White Bunny Ear Flowers

Make eight bunny ears, using $\frac{1}{6}$-length white strips. Glue a $\frac{3}{8}$" (1 cm) -long light green strip to each for stems.

Leaves

Make sixteen marquises with single curved end, using $\frac{1}{5}$-length light green strips.

Wreath Frame

Make a $2\frac{1}{4}$" (5.7 cm) -diameter frame by winding an olive green strip four times.

Butterfly

To make the body of a butterfly, roll a marquise, using a $\frac{1}{4}$-length yellow strip. Make two triangles, using full-length yellow strips for the upper wings. Make two triangles, using $\frac{2}{3}$-length canary yellow strips for the bottom wings. Glue the wings to the body and add antennae.

Assembly

1. Glue the wreath frame in the center of the card. Glue the canary yellow teardrop flowers and white bunny ear flowers proportionally around the wreath.

2. Glue the leaves between the flowers and glue the butterfly in the center.

See pattern on page 113.

Mother's Day

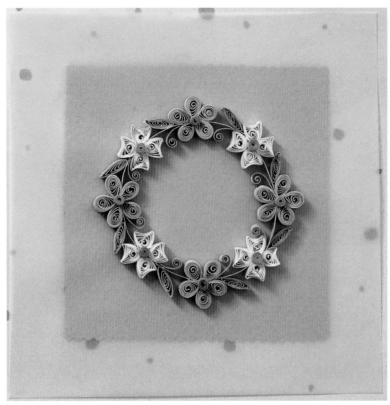

Size: 5" × 5" (12.5 × 12.5 cm)

LAVENDER TEARDROP FLOWERS

Make four flowers. For each flower, make five teardrops, using $1/3$-length lavender strips. Then roll a tight coil, using a $1/8$-length canary yellow strip, and glue it to the flower center.

WHITE BUNNY EAR FLOWERS

Make four flowers. For each flower, make four bunny ears, using $1/3$-length white strips. Make tight coils, using $1/8$-length canary yellow strips, and glue them to the flower centers.

LEAVES AND STEMS

Make eight marquises with single curved end, using $1/4$-length kiwi strips. Make stems, using $1/2$" (1.3 cm) -long light green strips.

VINES

Make eight vines, using $1/16$-length yellow strips.

ASSEMBLY

1. Glue four lavender flowers to form a 2" (5.1 cm) -diameter circle.

2. Glue the white bunny ear flowers between the lavender flowers, and add the stems.

3. Glue the leaves and vines.

Mother's Day

Thank You

Size: 5" × 5" (12.5 × 12.5 cm)

WHITE TEARDROP FLOWER

Make one flower with six teardrops, using ½-length white strips. Make a tight coil, using a ¼-length canary yellow strip, and glue it to the flower center. Make three teardrops, using ¼-length light green strips, and two loose scrolls, using ⅛-length yellow strips.

TURQUOISE BUNNY EAR FLOWER

Make one flower with four bunny ears, using ½-length turquoise strips. Make a tight coil, using a ¼-length white strip, and glue it to the flower center. Make two marquises, using ¼-length light green strips, and two loose scrolls, using ⅛-length white strips.

CANARY YELLOW MARQUISE FLOWER

Make eight marquises, using ½-length canary yellow strips. Make a tight coil, using a ⅓-length sage green strip, and glue it to the flower center. For a stem, prepare one 2⅛" (5.4 cm) -long olive green strip and curve it slightly. Make two marquises, each using ½-, ⅓-, and ¼-length moss green strips.

ASSEMBLY

1. Glue 2" x 2" (5.1 × 5.1 cm) pieces of light yellow and jade paper on the left side of the card and a 4½" × 2" (11.3 × 5.1 cm) piece of lilac paper on the right side.

2. Using spray glue, glue a 4½" × 4½" (11.5 × 11.5 cm) piece of tracing paper on top of the pieces in step 1.

3. Glue the white teardrop flower on the light yellow piece of paper. Glue the turquoise bunny ear flower on the jade piece of paper. Add the leaves and vines.

4. Glue the canary yellow flower on the lilac paper, and glue the leaves and stem.

Happy Birthday II

Size: 5" × 5" (12.5 × 12.5 cm)

FRINGED FLOWERS

Make two fringed flowers. For each flower, fringe ¼" (6 mm) -wide by 7⅞" (20 cm) -long bright blue strips, roll tightly, and glue the end. Spread out the fringed ends.

TURQUOISE TEARDROP FLOWERS

Make four flowers. Make each flower with five teardrops, using ⅓-length turquoise strips. Make tight coils, using 1/16" (1.6 mm) -wide ⅛-length yellow strips, and glue them to the flower centers.

FLOWER BUDS AND STEMS

Make four flower buds, using ¼-length lavender strips, and prepare four 1⅝" (4 cm) -long olive green strips for stems.

LIGHT PURPLE BUNNY-EAR FLOWERS AND LEAVES

Make eight bunny ears, using ¼-length light purple strips. Make eight marquises, using ¼-length moss green strips.

LARGE LEAVES AND VINES

Make two leaves. For each leaf, make three teardrops, using ⅓-length olive green strips. Make eight loose scrolls, using ⅙-length olive green and turquoise strips.

POLLEN

Stick canary yellow paper to a piece of double-sided tape and cut out ten triangles.

ASSEMBLY

1. Glue one of the fringed flowers on the upper left side and the other on the bottom right side.

2. Glue the four flower buds and stems to each side of the fringed flowers. Add the bunny ear flowers and vines.

3. Glue the turquoise teardrop flowers on each side of the fringed flowers. Add the large leaves and vines.

4. Finish with the pollen.

SEE PATTERN ON PAGE 113.

Anniversary

Size: 5" × 5" (12.5 × 12.5 cm)

CANARY YELLOW TEARDROP FLOWERS

Make two flowers. For each flower, make eight elongated teardrops, using $\frac{1}{3}$-length canary yellow strips. Then roll a tight coil, using a $\frac{1}{4}$-length yellow strip and glue it to the flower center.

YELLOW TEARDROP FLOWERS

Make four flowers. For each flower, make five teardrops, using $\frac{1}{3}$-length yellow strips. Then roll a tight coil, using a $\frac{1}{4}$-length orange strip, and glue it to the center of the flower.

CANARY YELLOW FLOWER BUDS

Make two flowers. For each flower, make three marquises with single curved end, using $\frac{1}{4}$-length canary yellow strips. Make bunny ears, using $\frac{1}{4}$-length moss green strips for flower cups.

WHITE FLOWERS WITH CENTER

Make six flowers. For each flower, make a tight coil with a $\frac{1}{2}$-length yellow strip and wrap it twice with a fringed $\frac{3}{16}$" (4.8 mm) -wide white strip.

WIDE LEAVES

Make two wide leaves with three small leaves each. For each

small leaf, make three marquises, using $\frac{1}{4}$-length moss green strips and glue them together. Glue three small leaves together to make one wide leaf.

LEAVES

Make two leaves. For each leaf, make three marquises with double curved ends, using $\frac{1}{3}$-length moss green strips and glue them together.

ASSEMBLY

1. Draw a 2 $\frac{1}{2}$" (6.4 cm) -diameter circle in the center.

2. Glue the two canary teardrop flowers facing each other. Make two groups of three white flowers and glue them facing each other.

3. Glue two yellow teardrop flowers to one side of each of the three white flower groups. Add the wide leaves next to the flowers.

4. Glue stems to the flower buds and position them between the canary yellow and white flowers.

5. Make the letters "LOVE" and glue them to the center.

SEE PATTERN ON PAGE 113.

Flower

Before I spoke his name
he was simply
one set of gestures, nothing more.

Then I spoke his name,
he came to me
and became a flower.

Just as I spoke his name,
I hope that someone will speak my name,
one right for my color and perfume.
I long to go to him
and become his flower.

We all of us
long to become something.
You for me, and I for you,
we long to become a
never-to-be-forgotten gaze.

Decorative Borders and Plaques

Family photos or photos of your children decorated with oval-shaped frames are guaranteed to produce smiles every time you look at them. It doesn't matter if the pictures are old or faded, these qualities will enhance the overall piece when combined with your quilling.

Bunnies in the Meadow

Various techniques are applied in this project. This quill work requires some experience, combining two shapes to form teardrop flowers, however, anyone can take on this challenge.

Size: 7⅞" × 6¼" (20 × 16 cm)

WHITE TEARDROP FLOWERS

Make five flowers. For each flower, make nine teardrops, using ⅓-length white strips. Make fringed flowers, using yellow ⅛" (3 mm) -wide and 2¾" (7 cm) -long strips. Glue a fringed flower to the center of each flower.

RABBIT FACE AND BODY

Make the face with a fringed flower, using a ¼" (6 mm) -wide 1½" (40 cm)-length white strip. Make the body with a fringed flower, using two ¼" (6 mm) -wide 2½" (67 cm)-length white strips. Glue the face to the body.

EARS

Roll a marquise, using a ¼-length pink strip, and continue rolling with a ⅓-length white strip. Pinch one end to make a marquise with single curved end. Glue the ears to the top of the face.

LEGS

Make four off-center marquises, using ⅗-length white strips. Attach to the bodies.

HAIR ORNAMENT, EYES, AND MOUTHS

Make a hair ornament with four teardrops, using $\frac{1}{16}$" (1.6 mm) -wide and $\frac{3}{4}$" (1.9 cm) -long red strips. Roll a tight coil, using a yellow strip and glue it to the center of the hairpin. Cut paper in the shape of mouths and eyes. Glue them to the faces.

STEMS WITH LEAVES

Make four stems with leaves. For each one, prepare a $5\frac{1}{8}$" (13 cm) - long kiwi strip and roll a teardrop, using only $3\frac{1}{2}$" (9 cm). Use the remaining $1\frac{5}{8}$" (4 cm) as the stem. Make four teardrops with $\frac{1}{2}$-length kiwi strips, eight with $\frac{1}{3}$-length kiwi strips, and four with $\frac{1}{4}$-length kiwi strips. Glue the teardrops to the stems according to size.

WIDE LEAVES

Make four marquises with double curved ends, using $\frac{1}{2}$-length moss green strips. Make three more with $\frac{1}{3}$-length moss green color strips. Make six wide leaves as shown.

CUT-OUT LEAVES

Fold a light green $\frac{3}{4}$" (1.9 cm) -wide strip in half lengthwise. Make about twenty-five leaves in various sizes. (See page 77.)

ASSEMBLY

1. Glue the cut-out leaves on the upper part.

2. Glue five white flowers on top of the leaves and add two stems with leaves on each side.

3. Glue the six wide leaves on the bottom part and position the two rabbits in the center.

70% of actual size

Medley of Flowers

Various techniques are applied in this project. While this quillwork requires some experience, combining two shapes to form teardrop flowers, anyone can take on this project.

Size: 7⅞" × 6¼" (20 × 16 cm)

WHITE FLOWERS WITH TWO SHAPES

Make three flowers. For each flower, make two off-center half-moons, using ½-length white strips and make a three-loop husking. Glue one half-moon to each side of the husking and wrap the entire petal twice with a white strip. Make a tight coil, using a ¼-length yellow strip, and wrap it twice with a light green strip. Glue it to the center of the flower.

PURPLISH BLUE TEARDROP FLOWERS

Make four flowers. For each flower, make six teardrops, using ½-length purplish blue strips. Then roll a tight coil, using a ¼-length canary yellow strip, and wrap it with a navy blue strip twice. Glue the coil to the center of the flower.

PURPLE FLOWERS WITH CENTERS

Make two flowers. For each flower, roll a tight coil, using a ¼-length canary yellow strip. Glue a fringed ¼" (6 mm) -wide ½-length purple strip to the tight coil and continue rolling. Spread the fringed ends.

PINK BUNNY EAR FLOWERS

Make three flowers each in pink and light pink. For each flower, make four bunny ears, using $\frac{1}{2}$-length pink or light pink strips. Then roll a tight coil, using a $\frac{1}{2}$-length white strip, and glue it to the center of the flower.

FRINGED FLOWERS

Make fringed flowers, using purplish blue $\frac{1}{4}$" (6 mm) -wide full-length strips.

WHITE FLOWERS MADE WITH A PUNCH TOOL

Prepare thirty-five white circles, using a punch tool. Make seven flowers. For each flower, glue one white circle onto a plastic sheet and, using tweezers, glue four more circles around it. Glue a $\frac{1}{16}$" (1.6 mm) -diameter yellow circle to the center of the flower.

LEAVES

Make twelve moss green leaves. For each leaf, make three marquises with single curved end, using $\frac{1}{3}$-length moss green strips.

Make four leaves. For each leaf, make one marquise, using a $\frac{1}{3}$-length kiwi strip, and another with a $\frac{1}{4}$-length strip, and glue them together. Make four leaves. For each leaf, roll two marquises, using $\frac{1}{3}$-length olive green strips, and three more, using $\frac{1}{4}$-length olive green strips. Glue them together.

ASSEMBLY

1. Glue the white flowers made with two shapes in the center.

2. Glue the purplish blue flowers on the left side of the white flowers. Glue the pink flowers on the right side to create a three-dimensional look.

3. Glue the purple flowers with centers in the space below the white flowers. Add the purple fringed flowers to the empty space above them.

4. Glue the white flowers made with the punch tool and the leaves in the spaces as shown in the picture.

90% of actual size

Decorative Marquise Flower Border

Using marquises, anyone can easily decorate framed photographs or beautiful poems.

Flower

Before I spoke his name
he was simply
one set of gestures, nothing more.

Then I spoke his name,
he came to me
and became a flower.

Just as I spoke his name,
I hope that someone will speak my name,
one right for my color and perfume.
I long to go to him
and become his flower.

We all of us
long to become something.
You for me, and I for you,
we long to become a
never-to-be-forgotten gaze.

Size: 7⁷⁄₈" × 6¹⁄₄" (20 × 16 cm)

Large Pink Marquise Flowers

Make six large flowers one each with pink, bright purple, purple, slate purple, light purple, and bluish purple strips. For each flower, make eight marquises, using $\frac{1}{2}$-length strips. Roll one yellow, one sky blue, two tangerine, and two bright sky blue tight coils, using $\frac{1}{3}$-length strips. Glue one coil to the center of each flower.

Medium Lavender Marquise Flowers

Make two flowers. For each flower, roll six marquises, using $\frac{1}{3}$-length lavender strips. Then roll a tight coil, using a $\frac{1}{4}$-length yellow or blue strip, and glue it to the center of the flower.

Small Light Purple Marquise Flowers

Make four flowers. For each flower, roll six marquises, using $\frac{1}{4}$-length lavender and light purple strips. Then roll a tight coil, using a $\frac{1}{5}$-length white strip, and glue it to the center of the flower.

Leaves

Make ten marquises, using $\frac{1}{4}$-length moss green strips, and six more with $\frac{1}{3}$-length strips.

Vines

Make eight loose scrolls, using $\frac{1}{4}$-length moss green strips, and two more with $\frac{1}{8}$-length strips.

White Flower Buds

Make two flower buds. For each one, roll three marquises, using $\frac{1}{4}$-length white strips. Make two more marquises, using $\frac{1}{4}$-length light purple strips.

Flower Cups

Make two V scrolls, using $\frac{1}{8}$-length moss green strips.

Cut-out Leaves

Fold a green $\frac{3}{8}$" (1 cm) -wide full-length strip in half lengthwise. Cut out ten leaf shapes.

Assembly

1. On each side of the frame, glue two large flowers and one medium lavender flower to form a triangle. Glue the remaining large flowers on top.

2. Add the leaves and vines. Glue the light purple marquise flowers between them.

3. Glue the flower buds and finish by adding pollen.

90% of actual size

Decorative Flower Border

This project is constructed with flowers and leaves made with different-size marquises of the same color family. It is suitable for decorating framed photographs or sayings.

Size: 7⁷⁄₈" × 6¹⁄₄" (20 × 16 cm)

Red-Orange Marquise Flowers in Full Boom

Make two flowers. For each flower, make seven marquises with single curved end, using $\frac{1}{2}$-length red-orange strips. Then roll a tight coil, using a $\frac{1}{4}$-length yellow strip, and glue it to the center of the flower. Make stamens by rolling half the length of a $\frac{1}{32}$ (0.8 mm) -wide and $\frac{3}{4}$" (1.9 cm) -long yellow strip. Make five stamens for each flower.

Marquise Flowers in Pastel Purple Tones

Make three marquises with $\frac{1}{8}$-length pastel purple strips, two marquises with $\frac{1}{7}$-length lavender strips, and two marquises each with $\frac{1}{6}$-length grape purple and lavender strips. Glue them according to size and color to a $1\frac{3}{4}$" (4.5 cm) -long moss green strip, as shown. Make four flowers.

Purple Fringed Flowers with Centers

Roll a tight coil, using a $\frac{1}{2}$-length rust color strip. Fringe a lavender $\frac{5}{16}$" (8 mm) -wide $\frac{1}{2}$-length strip and continue rolling around the tight coil.

Flower Buds

Make four flower buds. For each bud, make one teardrop, using a $\frac{1}{2}$-length lavender strip. Fold a $1\frac{1}{4}$" (3 cm) -long moss green strip in half and roll the ends outward. Glue the teardrop inside the moss green strip.

Leaves

Make four marquises, using $\frac{1}{4}$-length moss green strips, and eighteen more with $\frac{1}{3}$-length strips. Glue the marquises to $3\frac{1}{4}$" (8.25 cm) -long and 4" (10 cm) -long moss green strips, as shown in the picture.

Leaves Made with Huskings

Make a three-loop husking, using a grass green strip. Add one more loop, using a moss green strip.

Ribbon

Make two arrowheads, using full-length yellow strips, and glue them facing each other. Wrap the center once with a $\frac{1}{8}$" (3 mm) -wide yellow strip. Fold a $2\frac{3}{4}$" (7 cm) -long yellow strip in half, curl the ends, and glue it to the center of the ribbon.

Assembly

1. Glue the red-orange flowers; one on the upper left and the other on the lower right.

2. Glue the purple-tone marquise flowers on each side of the red-orange flowers, and add the purple fringed flowers.

3. Using the purple fringed flowers as guides, glue the leaves and the ribbons toward the center of each flower group.

80% of actual size

Decorative Portrait Border

In this project, an old family picture full of memories is framed and decorated with cut-out flowers, marquises, and tight coils.

Size: 7⅞" × 6¼" (20 × 16 cm)

LARGE AND SMALL CUT-OUT FLOWERS

Copy or draw the template shape onto light purple and grape purple paper. Cut out sixteen petals. (See page 49 for how to make cut-out flowers). Fringe the edges of the petals with short and long cuts. Slightly fold the bottom end of the petals back and spread the fringed edges outward. Using small tweezers, glue six of the petals to a small circle, and glue six more petals on top of them. Continue, adding four more petals. Make fringed flowers, using $3/16$" (4.8 mm) -wide $1/2$-length and $5/8$-length strips. Glue them to the centers of the large and small flowers.

PINK MARQUISE WITH CENTER HOLE FLOWERS

Make four flowers. For each flower, use an awl to make six tight marquises with center hole, using $1/2$-length pink strips. Make a tight coil, using a $1/16$" (1.6 mm) -wide $1/4$-length yellow strip, and glue it to the center of the flower.

PURPLISH BLUE TEARDROP FLOWERS

Make four flowers. For each flower, make six teardrops, using $1/3$-length purplish blue strips. Then roll a tight coil with a $1/4$-length tangerine strip and glue it to the center of the flower.

PURPLE AND WHITE BUNNY EAR FLOWERS

Make two purple and two white flowers. For each flower, make four bunny ears, using $1/3$-length strips. Then roll a tight coil, using a $1/8$-length yellow strip, and glue it to the center of the flower.

WHITE TIGHT-COIL FLOWERS

Use a needle tool to roll seven tight coils, using $1/8$-length white strips. Glue them together to make a flower. Make four flowers.

WHITE LEAVES WRAPPED IN GREEN

Make a marquise, using a $1/4$-length white strip. Wrap it once, using a light green strip, leaving $5/8$" (1.6 cm) for a stem. Glue five stems together to make one leaf. Make a total of four. Glue the vines to the base of the leaves.

TEARDROP AND CUT-OUT LEAVES

Make eight teardrops, using $1/3$-length moss green strips. Fold a $3/4$" (1.9 cm) -wide by 4" (10 cm) -long olive green strip in half lengthwise. Cut six leaves.

ASSEMBLY

1. Glue the large purple cut-out flower to the upper center. Place the small light purple flowers on each side of the purple flower.

2. Glue the pink marquise flowers on each side of the cut-out flowers, and add leaves.

3. Glue the purplish blue teardrop flowers in the spaces between and above the cut-out flowers. Fill in the empty areas with the white tight-coil flowers.

4. Glue the cut-out leaves and teardrop leaves around the flowers.

5. Arrange the lower area, using the same method.

SEE PATTERN ON PAGE 112.

Floral Wall Hanging Decoration
Sweet Home

Create a sweet home atmosphere by displaying a beautiful wooden plaque decorated with teardrops and marquises with center-hole flowers on your child's door.

Size: 6¼" × 4¾" (16 × 12 cm)

RIBBON

Make two arrowheads, using full-length lavender strips, and make two more with ⅔-length strips. Glue the arrowheads together and wrap the center with a ⅛" (3 mm) -wide strip.

PINK TEARDROP FLOWERS

Make six flowers. For each flower, use a needle tool to roll five tight coils with center holes, using ⅙-length dusty pink strips. Make tight coils, using ¾" (1.9 cm) -long tangerine strips. Glue five dusty pink tight coils around one tangerine tight coil.

TANGERINE BUNNY EAR

Make two bunny ears, using ⅙-length tangerine strips.

LEAVES AND STEMS (UPPER)

Make fifteen marquises, using ¼-length moss green strips. Prepare two 2⅛" (5.4 cm) -long moss green strips. Curve the strips to make elongated S shapes.

Lilac Marquise Flower

Make a flower with six marquises, using $\frac{1}{3}$-length lilac strips. Roll a tight coil, using a $\frac{1}{8}$-length white strip, and glue it to the center of the flower.

Lavender Marquise Flowers

Make two flowers. For each flower, make six marquises, using $\frac{1}{4}$-length lavender strips. Then roll a tight coil, using a $\frac{1}{8}$-length tangerine strip, and glue it to the center of the flower.

Leaves, Stems, and Vines (Bottom)

Make eleven marquises, using $\frac{1}{4}$-length moss green strips. Curve two $1\frac{5}{8}$" (4 cm) -long strips to make elongated S shapes. Make four loose scrolls, using $\frac{1}{4}$-length moss green strips.

Flower Buds

Make two flower buds. For each one, roll three teardrops, using $\frac{1}{4}$-length dusty pink strips.

Letters

Make letters with purple, moss green, cream, pink, and lavender strips.

Assembly

1. Glue the ribbon in the upper center and add the elongated S shape stems on each side.

2. Glue the leaves to the stems and add three dusty pink teardrop flowers on each side.

3. Glue the tangerine bunny ear flowers between leaves.

4. Glue the large flower in the lower center and glue the small flowers on each side of the large flower. Glue the two elongated S shape stems to each side and add the flower buds.

5. Glue the leaves and vines to the stems.

90% of actual size

Door Plaque Decorated with Butterfly and Flowers

Welcome

This decorative door plaque uses handmade letters along with white flowers and a butterfly to greet visitors with its simple message in springtime colors. Making the letters can be tricky, but you can learn this skill quickly by practicing a few times.

Size: 6¼" × 4¾" (16 × 12 cm)

WHITE TEARDROP FLOWER WITH A YELLOW CENTER

Roll eight tight coils, using ⅟₁₆-length yellow strips, and glue them together to make a flower center. Make seven teardrops, using ⅓-length white strips, and glue them around the flower center.

WHITE TEARDROP FLOWERS

Make two flowers. For each one, make eight teardrops with ¼-length white strips. Then roll a tight coil, using a ¼-length canary yellow strip, and glue it to the center of the flower.

YELLOW TEARDROP FLOWERS

Make two flowers. For each one, make five teardrops with ¼-length yellow strips. Then roll a tight coil, using a ⅛-length cream strip, and glue it to the center of the flower.

WHITE FLOWERS WITH FLOWER CENTERS

Make three fringed flowers. For each one, roll a tight coil, using a ½-length light cabbage green strip. The fringe ¼" (6 mm) -wide strip and wrap it twice around the tight coil.

YELLOW STEMS WITH TIGHT COILS

Make two stems with tight coils. For each one, roll four tight coils, using ⅛-length yellow strips, and glue them to a yellow ¾" (1.9 cm) -long strip.

CUT-OUT LEAVES

Fold a $\frac{3}{4}$" (2 cm) -wide and 4" (10 cm) -long moss green strip in half lengthwise and cut out 10 leaves in various sizes.

LEAVES AND VINES

Make four marquises, using $\frac{1}{4}$-length kiwi strips, and four loose scrolls, using 1 $\frac{1}{8}$" (3 cm) -long strips.

BUTTERFLY

Glue a $\frac{1}{16}$-length dark navy blue strip and a $\frac{1}{2}$-length canary yellow strip together. For the upper wings, begin rolling a tight coil from the dark navy blue end then continue rolling the canary yellow portion and form a triangle shape. For the lower wings, make two triangles with $\frac{1}{3}$-length yellow strips.

LETTERS

Make the letters "Welcome" using blue, purple, canary yellow, yellow, lavender, light green, and light blue strips.

ASSEMBLY

1. Glue the white flower with yellow center to the upper center. Glue the white teardrop flowers and the yellow teardrop flowers on each side.

2. Glue the stems between the flowers then add the leaves and vines.

3. Glue the fringed white flowers to the lower center. Add yellow stems with tight coils to each side.

4. Glue the cut-out leaves around the white fringed flowers.

5. Glue the butterfly and letters to the center.

Actual size

Christmas Wreaths and Snowflakes

Wreaths, poinsettias, candles, bells, ribbons, and snowflakes all add to the Christmas spirit and make the holiday season even merrier. Nothing creates a special holiday atmosphere better than decorating your home with the projects found in this section.

Christmas Square Wreath with Poinsettia and Bells

Create a unique atmosphere by displaying this green square frame decorated with a red paper ribbon. Spread the Christmas spirit by hanging these frames on doors or walls.

Size: 3½" × 3½" (8.9 × 8.9 cm)

HOLLY LEAVES

Make seven holly leaves, using ½-length olive green strips, and glue them together. Roll four tight coils, using ⅛-length red strips, and glue them to the center of the holly leaves.

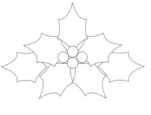

CANDLE

Make a cylinder, using one gold ⅝" (1.6 cm) -wide by 1" (2.5 cm) -long piece of paper. Make a marquise with single curved end, using a ⅓-length yellow strip, and wrap it twice with a canary yellow strip to make a flame.

BELLS

Glue three full-length gold strips together and roll a tight coil. Push out the center to form a bell shape. Make two bells and glue them together. (See page 23.)

RIBBON

Make a ribbon, using two red strips painted with gold; one ¼" (6 mm) -wide by 1⅜" (3.5 cm) -long, and the other ¼" (6 mm) -wide by 1⅝" (4 cm) -long. (See pages 43 and 51.)

SQUARE FRAME

Prepare a 2½" × 2½" (6.4 × 6.4 cm) green paper sheet and cut a 1¾" × 1¾" (4.5 × 4.5 cm) square from the center. Paint both edges of three 3/16" (4.8 mm) -wide full-length red strips gold. Wind the square frame with the red and gold strips, as shown in the picture.

ASSEMBLY

1. Glue the bells and the ribbon to the upper part of the frame and add the holly leaves and the candle to the bottom.

SEE PATTERN ON PAGE 115.

Christmas Wreath with Ribbon and Bells

In this project, make a wreath by gluing multiple marquises together and accenting it with a bell. This makes a nice wall hanging that you can use for years to come.

Size: 4" × 4" (10 × 10 cm)

GREEN WREATH

Make about forty-eight marquises with single curved end, using full-length olive green strips. Make a 2 ³/₄" (7 cm) -diameter circle by gluing four olive green strips together. Glue twenty-two of the marquises at slight angles inside the circle, and glue twenty-six on the outside.

YELLOW BERRIES

Use a needle tool to roll three tight coils, using ¹/₆-length yellow strips. Glue the coils together to make one berry. Make eight berries.

RIBBON STRIP

Connect two ³/₁₆" (4.8 mm) -wide full-length red strips together and paint the edges gold.

BELLS

Glue four full-length gold strips together and roll a tight coil. Make two bells. (See page 23.)

SMALL RIBBON

Prepare red strips with gold painted edges. Fold a ¹/₄" (6 mm) -wide by 1³/₄" (4.5 cm) -long strip and a ¹/₄" (6 mm) -wide by 2" (5.1 cm) -long strip in half. Mark the center at the folded line. For each strip, glue both ends to the center. Cut the center of the bottom layer and bend both ends down. Glue the upper and bottom layers of the ribbon together and wrap the center once with a ¹/₈" (3 mm) -wide red strip.

ASSEMBLY

1. Wind the gold painted red strip around the green wreath eight times. Glue the yellow berries in the spaces between the wound strip.

2. Glue the two gold bells to the top of the wreath and decorate with the small red ribbon.

Christmas Poinsettia and Candles

Holly leaves and candles made with wide paper are such
wonderful materials for decorating Christmas cards.

Size: 4" × 5⅛" (10 × 13 cm)

POINSETTIA

Make ten marquises with single
curved ends, using three ¾-length,
three ⅔-length, and four ½-length
bright red strips. Make four tight coils, using ⅙-length canary
yellow strips. Glue the coils to the center of the flower.

HOLLY LEAVES

Make twelve holly leaves with full-length olive green strips,
and glue them together as shown in the picture.

CANDLE AND FLAME

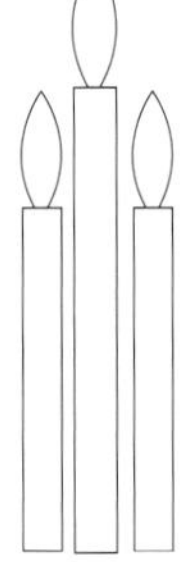

Prepare one 2" × 1⅝" (5.1 × 4 cm) and two 1⅝" ×
1⅝" (4 × 4 cm) pieces of gold paper. Glue each of
them to form ¼" (6 mm) -diameter candles. Roll a
marquise, using a ½-length yellow strip, and wrap
it twice with a canary yellow strip to make a flame
for the large candle. Roll two marquises, using ⅓-
length yellow strips, and wrap each of them twice with
canary yellow strips to make flames for the small candles.

BERRIES

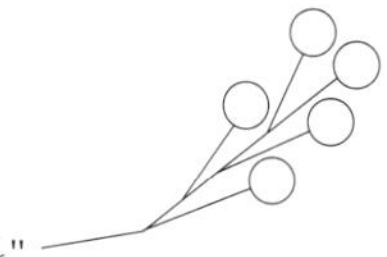

Roll tight coils, using ⅙-length red, yellow,
canary yellow, lavender, and purplish blue
strips. Make two of each color. Make two
stems with berries. For each one, glue a ³⁄₁₆"
(4.8 mm) -long brown stem to each coil,
then glue five of these to a 1¼" (3 cm) -long brown stem.

ASSEMBLY

1. Glue the holly leaves to the bottom and glue three
candles above them.

2. Glue the poinsettia on top of the holly leaves and add
berries on each side.

SEE PATTERN ON PAGE 114.

Spiral Christmas Wreath with Bells

This wreath, made with spiral shapes, creates a unique and colorful holiday wall hanging.

Size: 4⅛" × 4⅛" (10.5 × 10.5 cm)

GREEN WREATH

Prepare six long strips by connecting one full-length and one ½-length green strip together. Make six spiral shapes, using a needle tool, and glue all six together on one end. Twist all six spirals together to form one large spiral. Glue the ends together to form a 4" (10 cm) -diameter circle.

RIBBON STRIP

Prepare three ³⁄₁₆" (4.8 mm) -wide full-length red strips and paint both edges gold.

LARGE RIBBON WRAPPED IN GREEN STRIPS

Fold a ⅜" (1 cm) -wide by 4¾" (12 cm) -long red strip in half to find the center. Do the same with a 5⅛" (13 cm) -long red strip. Glue both ends to the center to make each layer of the ribbon. Wrap each red strip lengthwise with a green strip. Cut the center of the bottom layer ribbon, bend both ends down, and glue it to the upper ribbon layer. Wrap the center of the entire ribbon with a red strip. Prepare two ⅜" (1 cm) -wide by 1⅝" (4 cm) -long red strips, and cut a V shape out of each end. (See pages 43 and 51.)

GOLDEN BELLS

Connect three gold strips and make a tight coil. Shape the coil to form a bell shape. Make two bells. Roll tight coils, using ¹⁄₁₆" (1.6 mm) -wide by 5½" (14 cm) -long yellow strips, and attach one to the bottom of each bell.

SMALL RIBBON FOR BELLS

Use ¼" (6 mm) -wide by 1⅝" (4 cm) -long and ¼" (6 mm) by 1¾" (4.5 cm) -long red strips to make a small ribbon. Use the same method for making the large ribbon above.

ASSEMBLY

1. Wind the gold-painted red strip around the green wreath eight times.

2. Glue the two bells to the center of the wreath. Add the large ribbon to the top of the wreath.

SEE PATTERN ON PAGE 115.

Snowflakes

By doing these projects, you make maximum use of scrolls, one of the basic quilling shapes. Geometric shapes may be created through using the same shapes multiple times. Quilled snowflakes make wonderful additions to your Christmas decorations—consider displaying them on your tree.

Snowflake 1

Size: 2¼" × 2¼" (6 × 6 cm)

- eighteen ¼-length marquises
- twelve ⅙-length marquises
- eighteen ⅛-length marquises

ASSEMBLY

1. Make the center of the snowflake by gluing six ¼-length marquises together.

2. Prepare six 1" (2.5 cm) -long white strips and glue them to the center as shown in the picture.

3. Glue twelve ¼-length marquises close to the center. Glue twelve ⅙-length marquises to the center of the white strips.

4. Glue twelve ⅛-length marquises further from the center. Glue the remaining six marquises to the end of each strip.

SEE PATTERN ON PAGE 114.

Snowflake 2

Size: 2¾" × 2¾" (7 × 7 cm)

- eighteen ¼-length tight marquises with center holes made with a ⅛" (3 mm) -thick bamboo stick

- six ⅙-length tight coils with center holes made with a 1/16" (2 mm) -thick bamboo stick

- six ¼-length V scrolls

- six ⅛-length V scrolls

- six ¼-length V scrolls with glued middle

- twelve ⅙-length marquises

- twelve ⅛-length marquises

- six ⅕-length tight coils with center holes made with a 1/16" (2 mm) -thick/diameter bamboo stick

ASSEMBLY

1. Glue six ¼-length tight marquises with center hole together to make the center of the snowflake.

2. Glue six ⅙-length coils with center holes in between the marquises in step 1.

3. Glue one ¼-length tight marquise with center hole into each of six ¼-length V scrolls. Glue the scrolls to the marquises in step 2.

4. Glue the remaining ¼-length tight marquises to the center marquises.

5. Insert one ¼-length V scroll into each of the six ⅛-length V scrolls. Glue them to the marquises in step 4.

6. Glue two ⅙-length marquises to each side of the V scroll. Glue two ⅛-length marquises, one per tip, to each of the ⅛-length V scrolls.

7. Glue six ⅕-length tight marquises to the ends of each ⅙-length V scroll.

SEE PATTERN ON PAGE 115.

Snowflake 3

Size: 2¾" × 2¾" (7 × 7 cm)

- twelve ¼-length marquises
- six ¼-length closed hearts
- five ⅛-length tight marquises with center hole made with a ¹⁄₁₆" (1.6 mm) -thick bamboo stick and make six flowers each made with marquises with a center hole
- six ⅙-length V scrolls
- six ⅙-length V scrolls with glued middle
- six ⅛-length tight coils

ASSEMBLY

1. Glue a ¼-length marquise inside a closed heart. Make six of these and glue them together to form the center of the snowflake.

2. Glue ¼-length marquises between the closed hearts.

3. Connect six flowers to the closed hearts.

4. Glue ⅙-length V scrolls to each of the flowers. Connect ⅙-length V scrolls with glued middle.

5. Glue ⅛-length tight coils to the tips of the snowflake.

SEE PATTERN ON PAGE 115.

Snowflake 4

Size: 2½" × 2½" (6.5 × 6.5 cm)

- six ½-length diamonds
- six ⅙-length V scrolls
- twelve ⅙-length marquises
- six ¼-length V scrolls with glued middle
- thirty ⅙-length tight coils with center hole made with a ¹⁄₃₂" (0.8 mm) -thick needle tool

ASSEMBLY

1. Glue six ½-length diamonds together to form the center of the snowflake.

2. Glue ⅙-length V scrolls between the diamonds. Connect ¼-length V scrolls with glued middle inside the previous V scrolls.

3. Glue two ⅙-length marquises inside of each V scroll. Glue six ⅙-length tight coils to the points where the two V scrolls meet.

4. Glue four ⅙-length tight coils together and attach them to the tips of the snowflake.

SEE PATTERN ON PAGE 114.

Snowflake 5

Size: 3" × 3" (7.5 × 7.5 cm)

- six $\frac{1}{2}$-length angled marquises

- eighteen $\frac{1}{2}$-length diamonds

- twelve $\frac{1}{8}$-length C scrolls

- twelve $\frac{1}{8}$-length tight coils with center hole made using a $\frac{1}{32}$" (0.8 mm) -thick needle tool

- twelve $\frac{1}{6}$-length tight marquises with center hole made using a $\frac{1}{16}$" (1.6 mm) -thick needle tool

- twelve $\frac{1}{6}$-length uneven S scrolls

ASSEMBLY

1. Glue six $\frac{1}{2}$-length angled marquises together to form the center of the snowflake.

2. Connect six $\frac{1}{2}$-length diamonds to the angled marquises.

3. Attach C scrolls to each side of the point where the diamonds and angled marquises meet in step 2.

4. Glue diamonds between the C scrolls and connect $\frac{1}{6}$-length marquises.

5. Attach diamonds to the diamonds in step 2. Glue two $\frac{1}{8}$-length tight coils, one on each side of the point where the diamonds connect.

6. Glue $\frac{1}{6}$-length uneven S scrolls to the sides of the diamonds in step 5. Glue $\frac{1}{6}$-length tight coils to the tips of the snowflake.

SEE PATTERN ON PAGE 114.

Paper Picture Frames and Gift Boxes

When showing a loved one your graditude, why not send a handmade gift box decorated with your quilling? Or make a potpourri bag embellished with your designs—the recipient will be impressed and delighted.

Decorative Tight Marquise Paper Frame

This paper frame is designed for framing photos or poems, but it can also be used as a card. Basic shapes and techniques such as tight marquises, grape rolls, and vines are used to complete this project.

Size: 4⅛" × 5" (10.5 × 12.7 cm)

Large Tight Marquise Flowers

Make tight marquises, using a $\frac{1}{32}$"
(0.8 mm) -thick needle tool, and $\frac{1}{2}$-
length pastel purple, light green, blue,
pink, sky blue, and lavender strips.
Wrap each marquise twice with a
black strip. Push out the center and apply glue to the inside
of each marquise. Roll two tight coils, using $\frac{1}{3}$-length pastel
purple strips, and wrap each one twice with a black strip.
Push out the center and apply glue to the inside of each
coil. Glue six marquises around each tight coil to make
two flowers.

Small Tight Marquise Flowers

Make four flowers with tight teardrops, using
$\frac{1}{4}$-length strips of the same five pastel colors
used to make the large flowers above. Make
tight coils, using $\frac{1}{16}$" (1.6 mm) -wide by $\frac{3}{4}$" (1.9 cm) -long
white strips, and use as flower centers. (To create a three-
dimensional look, push out the center of each coil to form
grape rolls.)

Flower Buds

Make two flower buds. For each one, make
three tight teardrops, using $\frac{1}{3}$-length strips of
different pastel tones. Push out the center of
each roll and glue the inside.

Leaves

Make twelve tight marquises, using $\frac{1}{3}$-length light green
strips, and two more with $\frac{1}{4}$-length strips. Push out the center of each roll and glue the inside.

Vines and Stems

Make two loose scrolls, using $\frac{1}{4}$-length lavender strips, and six more with $\frac{1}{5}$-length strips.
Prepare two $1\frac{1}{4}$" (3 cm) -long strips by $1\frac{3}{4}$"
(4.5 cm) -long strips and make S shapes by
curling the ends.

Assembly

1. Glue one of the large tight marquise flowers on the
upper left side and the other one on the bottom right side.

2. Glue the lavender stems next to the large flower as
shown in the picture. Add the small tight marquise
flowers to either side of the stems.

3. Glue the leaves and vines and add the flower buds
between the small flowers to finish.

SEE PATTERN ON PAGE 112.

How to Make a Paper Frame

1. Copy the pattern and transfer it to the desired color of
paper by marking the corners with an awl then connect
the corners, using the awl or a pencil.

2. When using a pencil, erase the lines later. When using an
awl, it is sometimes difficult to see the markings.

3. Creases may be marked with an awl, using a ruler.
Creases make folding the paper easier.

4. Cut out a $1\frac{3}{4}$" × 2" (4.5 × 5.1 cm) square from the paper
for displaying a photo.

5. Make stitch marks on the edges of the paper with a
punch wheel.

SEE PATTERN ON PAGE 119.

How to Make a Potpourri Sachet

1–3. Follow steps 1, 2, and 3 for How to Make a Paper Frame,
above.

4. After making a potpourri bag, fold the sides of the front
and back, and punch holes in both sides of
the paper at the same time.

5. Put a cover on the top of the bag and punch two holes.
Make ribbons, using paper strips.

SEE PAGES 94–99 AND PATTERN ON PAGE 118.

Decorative Teardrop Paper Frame

This paper frame is also designed for displaying special photos, sayings, or poems. Basic shapes and techniques, such as bunny ears, teardrops, and elongated marquises, are used to decorate the frame. By using a punch wheel, you can create a unique leatherlike texture.

Size: 4⅛" × 5" (10.5 × 12.7 cm)

White Teardrop Flowers

Make two flowers. For each flower, roll nine teardrops, using $\frac{1}{4}$-length white strips. Then roll a tight coil, using a $\frac{1}{16}$" (1.6 mm) -wide $\frac{1}{5}$-length yellow strip, and glue it to the center of the flower.

Blue Bunny Ear Flowers

Make six flowers. For each flower, make three bunny ears, using $\frac{1}{3}$-length blue strips, and three teardrops, using $\frac{1}{7}$-length strips. Alternately glue the three bunny ears and three teardrops together. Then roll a tight coil, using a $\frac{1}{16}$" (1.6 mm) -wide $\frac{1}{5}$-length yellow strip, and glue it to the center of the flower.

Stem with Yellow Marquise Flowers

Make a stem by slightly curving a $\frac{3}{4}$" (1.9 cm) -long light green strip. Roll a tight coil, using a $\frac{1}{8}$-length yellow strip, and three tight marquises, using $\frac{1}{7}$-length strips. Glue the tight coil and three tight marquises to the stem. Make a total of four stems with flowers.

Yellow Tight Teardrop Flower Buds

Make two flower buds. For each flower bud, roll three tight teardrops, using $\frac{1}{4}$-length yellow strips.

Leaves

Make about twelve marquises, using $\frac{1}{8}$-, $\frac{1}{7}$-, and $\frac{1}{6}$-length yellow-green strips.

Assembly

Top

1. Glue the white flower in the center and add the bunny ear flowers on each side. Position and glue the stems with yellow flowers on each side.

2. Glue leaves to the white flower and to the stems with yellow flowers.

Bottom

1. Glue the white teardrop flower in the center and add two bunny ear flowers on each side.

2. Glue the stems with yellow flowers next to the bunny ear flowers and add the yellow flower buds on each side.

3. Glue leaves to the white flower, blue bunny ear flowers, and the stems with yellow flowers.

4. Stick double-sided tape to a piece of yellow paper and cut about seventeen triangles to make pollen. Glue the pollen around the flowers to decorate.

Potpourri Gift Sachets

Demonstrating various quilled shapes and techniques, this project has a uniquely timeless appeal.

Bouquet

Size: 4" × 6" (10 × 15 cm)

PINK BUNNY EAR FLOWERS

Make two pink and one light pink flower. For each flower, make four bunny ears, using ½-length strips. Then roll a tight coil, using a ½-length white strip, and push out the center to form a grape roll. Glue the grape roll to the center of the flower.

EMERALD GREEN TEARDROP FLOWERS

Make two flowers. For each one, make six teardrops by rolling a ⅓-length canary yellow and ⅓-length emerald strip together. Then roll a tight coil, using a ⅓-length canary yellow strip, and glue it to the center of the flower.

LEAVES AND VINES

Make three leaves. For each one, make three marquises, using ⅓-length yellow-green strips. Make three loose scrolls with ¼-length yellow strips.

LEAVES WITH A CURVED END

Make three marquises with single curved end, using ½-length olive green strips.

WHITE FLOWERS MADE WITH A PUNCH TOOL

Make four ¼" (6 mm) -diameter white flowers, using a flower-shaped punch tool. Punch ¹⁄₁₆" (1.6 mm) -diameter yellow circles with a circle punch tool, and use them as flower centers.

SEE PATTERNS ON PAGES 116 AND 118.

Flower Wreath

Size: 4" × 6" (10 × 15 cm)

PURPLE TEARDROP FLOWERS

Make three flowers. For each flower, roll six teardrops, using $\frac{1}{2}$-length purple strips. Then connect a 2" (5.1 cm) -long canary yellow strip to a 1$\frac{3}{4}$" (4.5 cm) -long grape purple strip, and roll a tight coil starting from the canary end. Glue the coil to the center of the flower.

GRAPE PURPLE TEARDROP FLOWERS

Make six flowers. For each flower, make five teardrops, using $\frac{1}{4}$-length grape purple strips. Wrap each teardrop twice with a light purple strip. Then glue a $\frac{1}{8}$-length light yellow strip and a $\frac{1}{8}$-length canary yellow strip together, and roll a tight coil starting from the light yellow end. Glue the coil to the center of the flower.

LEAVES

Make six teardrops, using $\frac{1}{4}$-length yellow-green strips.

CUT-OUT LEAVES

Fold a $\frac{3}{8}$" (1 cm) -wide by 4" (10 cm) -long olive green strip in half-lengthwise and cut out nine leaf shapes.

POLLEN

Make nine tight coils, using $\frac{3}{8}$" (1 cm) -long canary yellow strips.

SEE THE PATTERN ON PAGE 116.

Flower and Bee

Size: 4" × 6" (10 × 15 cm)

PUMPKIN ORANGE TEARDROP FLOWERS

Make three flowers with six teardrops each. For each teardrop, roll a ⅓-length pumpkin orange and a ⅓-length emerald green strip together. Then roll a tight coil, using a ⅓-length yellow strip and glue it to the center of each flower.

WHITE FLOWER WITH A CENTER

Make a tight coil, using a ¼-length light yellow strip. Glue a fringed ⁵⁄₁₆" (8 mm) -wide and 2" (5.1 cm) -long white strip to the tight coil and continue rolling.

BUDS

Make two teardrop buds, using ½-length pumpkin orange strips. Wrap each teardrop with an emerald green strip.

LEAVES AND VINES

Make five teardrops, using ½-length turquoise strips, and make four loose scrolls, using ¼-length grass green strips.

BEE

To make wings, roll two teardrops, using ½-length canary yellow strips. To make the head, roll a tight coil, using a ⅓-length black strip. Make a teardrop, using a ½-length black strip. and use it as the body.

SEE PATTERN ON PAGE 116.

May Roses

Size: 4" × 6" (10 × 15 cm)

WHITE TEARDROP FLOWERS

Make three flowers. For each flower, use a needle tool and full-length white strips to roll five tight teardrops. To make the flower centers, cut several short, thin pieces from a white strip ($1/32$" × $3/16$" [0.8 × 4.8 mm]) then punch small canary yellow circles, using a punch tool. Using tweezers, glue one thin white strip to each small circle to make a stamen. Make eight stamens per flower and glue them to the flower centers.

FOLDED PINK ROSE

Make three roses, using $3/8$" (1 cm) -wide by $10\,5/8$" (27 cm) -long pink strips. (See How to Make a Folded Rose on page 24.)

LEAVES

Make three leaves. For each leaf roll five marquises, using $1/3$-length khaki strips.

LEAVES MADE WITH A PUNCH TOOL

Punch three olive green leaves, using a rose leaf–shaped punch tool.

SEE PATTERN ON PAGE 116.

Wildflowers

Size: 4" × 6" (10 × 15 cm)

PURPLE TEARDROP FLOWER

Make a flower with six teardrops, using $\frac{1}{2}$-length lavender strips. Roll a tight coil, using a $\frac{1}{3}$-length yellow strip, and glue it to the center of the flower.

LEAVES AND STEM

Make two teardrops using $\frac{1}{3}$-length olive green strips and three teardrops, using $\frac{1}{2}$-length strips. Prepare a 2" (5.1 cm) -long moss green strip for a stem.

WHITE TEARDROP FLOWER

Make a tight coil, using a $\frac{1}{6}$-length moss green strip, and make five teardrops, using $\frac{1}{2}$-length white strips. Glue the five teardrops around the tight coil to make one flower.

LEAVES AND STEM

Prepare a 2$\frac{1}{2}$" (6.4 cm) -long light green strip for a stem. Make six marquises with single curved end, using $\frac{1}{3}$-length dusty green strips.

CANARY YELLOW MARQUISE FLOWER

Make a flower with seven irregular marquises, using $\frac{1}{2}$-length canary yellow strips. Roll a tight coil, using a $\frac{1}{3}$-length khaki strip, and glue it to the center of the flower.

LEAVES AND A STEM

Cut about twenty khaki strips of varying lengths, ranging from $\frac{1}{4}$" (6 mm) to $\frac{5}{8}$" (1.6 cm) -long. Glue the strips together to make four leaves as shown in the picture.

SEE PATTERN ON PAGE 116.

Flowers and Butterfly

Size: 4" × 6" (10 × 15 cm)

BLUE HUSKING FLOWER

Make a five-loop fan husking, using a 9" (23 cm) -long blue strip and wrap the entire husking three times. Use seven five-loop fan huskings to make one flower. Roll a tight coil, using a $\frac{1}{2}$-length lavender strip and shape it to form a grape roll. Glue the grape roll to the center of the flower.

TURQUOISE HUSKING FLOWERS

Make a three-loop fan husking, using a 6" (15.2 cm) -long turquoise strip, and wrap the entire husking three times. Make two flowers with seven three-loop fan huskings each. Roll tight coils, using $\frac{1}{2}$-length lilac strips and shape them to form grape rolls. Glue a grape roll to the center of each flower.

BUTTERFLY

For the upper wings, make two triangles, using $\frac{1}{2}$-length canary yellow strips. For the lower wings, make two triangles, using $\frac{1}{2}$-length dusty yellow strips. For the body, roll a mar-

quise, using a $\frac{1}{4}$-length dusty yellow strip. Make a V scroll, using a $\frac{1}{16}$" (1.6 mm) -wide by 1" (2.5 cm) -long dusty yellow strip, and use it as antennae.

LEAVES

Make three large leaves. For each leaf, make three four-loop vertical huskings, using $4\frac{1}{2}$" (11.4 cm) -long moss green strips. Make two smaller leaves with three three-loop vertical huskings, using $2\frac{1}{2}$" (6.4 cm) -long moss green strips.

FLOWERS MADE WITH A PUNCH TOOL

Punch out five $\frac{1}{4}$" (6 mm) -diameter yellow flowers, using a small flower-shaped punch. Stick a piece of canary yellow paper to double-sided tape and cut out small triangles. Glue them to the center of the flowers.

SEE PATTERN ON PAGE 116.

Gift Boxes

A gift presented in any of the boxes described in this section is bound to make a
lasting impression on the recipient. Express your hidden creativity by enhancing your gift box projects
with folded roses, marquise flowers, husking flowers, teardrops, bunny ears, and much more.

Oval Gift Box

Size: 4½" × 3" (11.5 × 7.5 cm)

NOTE: Decorate the lid of your gift box with beadwork or other decorative materials to make it even more elaborate.

Blue Folded Roses

Make three roses, using $\frac{3}{8}$" (1 cm) -wide by $10\frac{5}{8}$" (27 cm) -long blue and green-blue strips. (See How to Make a Folded Rose on page 24.)

Light Purple Teardrop Flowers

Make two flowers. For each flower, make six teardrops, using $\frac{1}{2}$-length light purple strips. Then roll a tight coil, using $\frac{1}{4}$-length canary yellow strip, wrap each one twice with a navy blue strip, and glue to the center of the flower.

Leaves

Make nine leaves. For each leaf, make three marquises, using $\frac{1}{4}$-length olive green, khaki, and dusty green strips.

Oval Box

To make the lid, cut a $4\frac{1}{2}$" × 3" (11.5 × 7.5 cm) oval and a $\frac{3}{8}$" (1 cm) -wide by $13\frac{3}{4}$" (34.4 cm) -long strip out of white corrugated cardboard. To make the base, cut another $4\frac{1}{2}$" × $2\frac{3}{4}$" (11.5 × 7.2 cm) oval and a $1\frac{3}{8}$" (3.5 cm) -wide × $15\frac{3}{4}$" (40 cm) -long strip. To assemble the parts, glue the $\frac{3}{8}$" (1 cm) -wide by $13\frac{3}{4}$" (35 cm) -long strip to the oval-shaped cutout for the lid. Make the base in the same way, but punch holes on one side of the bottom oval before gluing. Even though the box is based on a pattern, you can adjust the size according to the size of the gift.

Assembly

1. Glue three blue folded roses and two purple flowers to the center of the lid.

2. Glue olive green, khaki, and dusty green leaves around the flowers.

Box base

Box lid

Actual size

Square Gift Box

Size: 3¼" × 3¼" (8.5 × 8.5 cm)

PINK BUNNY EAR FLOWER

Make a flower with five bunny ears, using full-length pink strips. Make a tight coil, using a $\frac{1}{2}$-length white strip, and shape it to form a grape roll. Glue the grape roll to the center of the flower.

LARGE JADE GREEN FAN HUSKING FLOWER

Make a three-loop fan husking (longest loop is $\frac{5}{16}$" [8 mm] -long), using a 9" (23 cm) -long jade green strip, and wrap the entire husking three times. Make one flower by gluing seven fan huskings together. Roll a tight coil, using $\frac{1}{2}$-length lavender strip, and shape it to form a grape roll. Glue the grape roll to the center of the flower.

SMALL JADE GREEN FAN HUSKING FLOWER

Make one turquoise and one jade green flower. For each flower, make seven three-loop fan huskings (longest loop is $\frac{5}{16}$" [8 mm] -long), using 6" (15.2 cm) -long strips and wrapping each husking three times. Make a flower center, using the same method for the large jade green flower, but use a $\frac{1}{3}$-length lavender strip instead.

PINK FOLDED ROSES

Make folded roses, using $\frac{3}{8}$" (1 cm) -wide by $10\frac{5}{8}$" (27 cm) -long pink and light pink strips; make one rose of each color. (See How to Make a Folded Rose on page 24.)

LEAVES

Make five leaves. For each leaf, make three teardrops, using $\frac{1}{3}$-length moss green strips.

CUT-OUT LEAVES

Fold a $\frac{3}{4}$" (1.9 cm) -wide by 4" (10 cm) -long moss green strip in half lengthwise and cut out three leaves. Fringe the edges of the leaves. (See page 73.)

SQUARE BOX

To make the lid, cut a $3\frac{1}{4}$" × $3\frac{1}{4}$" (8.5 × 8.5 cm) square and a $\frac{3}{8}$" (1 cm) -wide by $15\frac{3}{4}$" (40 cm) -long strip out of a piece of white corrugated cardboard. To make the base, cut out a $3\frac{1}{4}$" × $3\frac{1}{4}$" (8.2 × 8.2 cm) square and a $1\frac{3}{8}$" × $15\frac{3}{4}$" (3.5 × 40 cm) strip. Glue the pieces together, using the same method for the oval box.

ASSEMBLY

1. Glue two roses, the large husking flower, and the smaller husking flowers around the center leaving some space in the middle.

2. Stick a piece of double-sided tape to the back of the pink bunny ear flower and add it to the center. Glue the cut-out leaves between the flowers.

3. Glue the teardrop leaves between the flowers.

Box base

Box lid

90% of actual size

Heart-Shaped Box

Size: 4" × 4" (10 × 10 cm)

TWO TONE YELLOW FLOWER

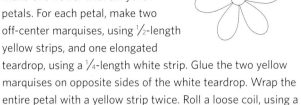

Make one flower with six yellow petals. For each petal, make two off-center marquises, using $\frac{1}{2}$-length yellow strips, and one elongated teardrop, using a $\frac{1}{4}$-length white strip. Glue the two yellow marquises on opposite sides of the white teardrop. Wrap the entire petal with a yellow strip twice. Roll a loose coil, using a $\frac{1}{3}$-length canary yellow strip. Glue it to the center of the flower.

CANARY YELLOW MARQUISE FLOWER

Make one flower with eight marquises. For each marquise, roll one $\frac{1}{4}$-length cream and one $\frac{1}{4}$-length canary yellow strip together. Roll three tight coils, using $\frac{1}{8}$-length light green strips, and glue them to the center of the flower.

WHITE BUNNY EAR FLOWER

Make one flower with five bunny ears, using $\frac{1}{2}$-length white strips. Roll a tight coil, using a $\frac{1}{3}$-length yellow strip, and shape it to form a grape roll. Glue the grape roll to the center of the flower.

PINK TEARDROP FLOWER

Make one flower with five teardrops, using $\frac{1}{3}$-length pink strips. Make a tight roll, using a $\frac{1}{6}$-length yellow strip, and glue it to the center of the flower.

CANARY YELLOW TEARDROP FLOWER

Make one flower with five teardrops, using $\frac{1}{4}$-length canary yellow strips. Make a tight roll, using a $\frac{1}{6}$-length moss green strip, and glue it to the center of the flower.

CREAM LILY OF THE VALLEY FLOWER

Make six lily of the valley shapes, using $\frac{1}{4}$-length cream strips. Glue them to a $1\frac{1}{4}$" (3 cm) -long yellow-green stem.

LEAVES AND POLLEN

Make four teardrops, using $\frac{1}{4}$-length moss green strips. Make seven tight coils, using $\frac{1}{8}$-length canary yellow strips.

HEART-SHAPED BOX

To make the lid, cut a 4" × 4" (10.2 × 10.2 cm) heart shape (use the pattern below) and a $\frac{3}{8}$" × $15\frac{3}{4}$" (1 × 40 cm) strip out of a white piece of corrugated cardboard. To make the base, cut a 4" × 4" (10 × 10 cm) square and a $1\frac{3}{8}$" × $15\frac{3}{4}$" (3.5 × 40 cm) strip. Glue the pieces together, using the same method for the oval box.

ASSEMBLY

1. Glue the two-tone yellow flower slightly below the center and glue the canary yellow marquise flower above it.

2. Glue the white bunny ear and lavender teardrop flowers on the right side of the two-tone yellow flower, Glue the canary yellow teardrop and lily of the valley to the left side of the yellow two-tone flower.

3. Decorate with leaves and pollen.

Box base

Box lid

80% of actual size

Place Cards

Make special occasions, such as weddings, more memorable by presenting place cards with your guests' names decorated with quilling. in this section, you will create uniquely designed place cards by applying all the quilling techniques including folding white or pastel roses.

Purplish Blue Marquise Flower and White Teardrop Flower

Size: 4" × 2½" (10 × 6.5 cm)

PURPLISH BLUE MARQUISE FLOWER

Make one flower. Using a $1/32$" (0.8 mm) -diameter needle tool, make six tight marquises with center holes, using $1/3$-length purplish blue strips. Glue a $1\frac{1}{4}$" (3.2 cm) -long yellow strip and a $1\frac{1}{4}$" (3.2 cm) -long grape purple strip together. Roll a tight coil, using the connected strip to make the flower center.

WHITE TEARDROP FLOWERS

Make two flowers. For each teardrop, roll five teardrops, using $1/3$-length white strips. Then roll a tight coil, using a $1/16$" (1.6 mm) -wide $1/8$-length tangerine strips, and glue it to the center of each flower.

PURPLISH BLUE TEARDROP FLOWERS

Make two purplish blue flowers and one dusty pink flower. For each one, use a $1/32$" (0.8 mm) -diameter needle tool, roll a tight teardrop with a center hole, using a $1/8$-length strip. Then roll a tight coil, using a $3/8$" (1 cm) -long canary yellow strip, and glue it to the center of the flower.

STEMS WITH LEAVES

Make four leaves. For each one, prepare a $1/4$-length moss green strip and roll a marquise from one end leaving $3/8$" (1 cm) unrolled. Then make four marquises, using $1/6$-length strips, and another four, using $1/8$-length strips. Glue the marquises around the flowers and stems.

SEE PATTERN ON PAGE 117.

Pink Rose and White Flowers

Size: 4" × 2½" (10 × 6.5 cm)

PINK FOLDED ROSES

Make one rose, using a ³⁄₈" (1 cm) -wide full-length pink strip. (See How to Make a Folded Rose on page 24.)

LEAVES FOR ROSES

Make two yellow-green leaves, using a leaf-shaped punch tool.

WHITE FLOWERS WITH CENTERS

Make tight coils, using ¼-length light green strips. Make a ¼" (6 mm) -wide by 1¾" (4.5 cm) -long fringed white strip. Glue the fringed strip to the coil and continue rolling. Spread the fringed edges.

FLOWER BUDS AND STEMS

Make two teardrops, using ¼-length dusty grape strips, and glue them to a ½" (1.3 cm) -long moss green strip.

LEAVES AND VINES

Make four marquises, using ¼-length moss green strips. Make two loose scrolls, using ⅛-length moss green strips.

SEE PATTERN ON PAGE 117.

Lavender and Purplish Blue Teardrop Flowers

Size: 4" × 2½" (10 × 6.5 cm)

PURPLISH BLUE TEARDROP FLOWER

Make a flower with six teardrops, using ½-length purplish blue strips. Glue a 2" (5.1 cm) -long canary yellow strip and a 1¾" (4.5 cm) -long grape purple strip together. Roll a tight coil, using the connected strip, and glue it to the center of the flower.

LAVENDER TEARDROP FLOWERS

Make two flowers. For each flower, make six teardrops, using ⅓-length lavender strips. Then roll a tight coil, using a ⅛-length canary yellow strip, and glue it to the center of the flower.

FLOWER BUDS

Make one flower bud with three teardrops. using ½-length lavender strips. Make a half-moon with a ⅓-length moss green strip, and use it as a flower cup.

STEMS WITH LEAVES

Prepare an olive green strip that is ⅝" (1.6 cm) longer than a ¼-length strip. Roll a tight marquise, using only ¼-length of the strip, and use the remainder as a stem.

LEAVES

Make four teardrops, using ¼-length olive green strips.

SEE PATTERN ON PAGE 117.

Pink Roses and Purple Teardrop Flowers

Size: 4" × 2½" (10 × 6.5 cm)

PINK FOLDED ROSES

Make one white and two pink folded roses, using ⅜" (1 cm) -wide full-length white strips. (See How to Make a Folded Rose on page 24.)

PURPLE TEARDROP FLOWERS

Make one flower with five teardrops, using ¼-length lavender strips. Make two more, using ¼-length dusty grape purple strips. Roll tight coils, using ⅛-length dusty yellow strips, and glue one to the center of each flower.

LEAVES FOR ROSES

Punch two leaves from a yellow-green paper strip, using a leaf-shaped punch tool.

LEAVES AND VINES

Make two marquises and two loose scrolls, using ⅛-length olive green strips.

SEE PATTERN ON PAGE 117.

Turquoise Marquise Flower and Grape Teardrop Flowers

Size: 4" × 2½" (10 × 6.5 cm)

TURQUOISE MARQUISE FLOWER

Make one flower with six marquises, using ⅓-length turquoise strips. Roll a tight coil, using a 1/16" (1.6 mm) -wide ¼-length canary yellow strip, and glue it to the center of the flower.

GRAPE TEARDROP FLOWERS

Make three flowers with five teardrops each. To make each teardrop, roll a ¼-length grape strip and wrap it twice with a dusty grape purple strip. Connect a ⅛-length yellow strip and a ⅛-length canary yellow strip, make a tight coil, and glue it to the center of the flower.

LEAVES AND VINES

Make seven teardrops, using ⅛-length olive green strips. Make four loose scrolls, using ⅛-length moss green strips.

SEE PATTERN ON PAGE 117.

Blue Marquise Flowers

Size: 4" × 2½" (10 × 6.5 cm)

BLUE MARQUISE FLOWER

Make a flower with six marquises, using ⅓-length blue strips. Roll a tight coil, using a 1/16" (1.6 mm) -wide ¼-length dusty yellow strip, and glue it to the center of the flower.

TURQUOISE MARQUISE FLOWERS

Make three flowers. For each flower, roll six marquises, using ¼-length turquoise strips. Then roll a tight coil, using a ⅕-length canary yellow strip, and glue it to the center of the flower.

FLOWER BUDS AND STEMS

Make two teardrops, using ¼-length lemon strips. Glue the teardrops to a ⅝" (1.6 cm) -long olive green stem.

LEAVES

Make four marquises, using ¼-length olive green strips.

SEE PATTERN ON PAGE 117.

Red Floral Bouquet, page 50

85% of actual size

Decorative Portrait Border, page 72

75% of actual size

Decorative Tight Marquise
Paper Frame, page 90

Actual size

Anniversary, page 61

Wishes and Love, page 56

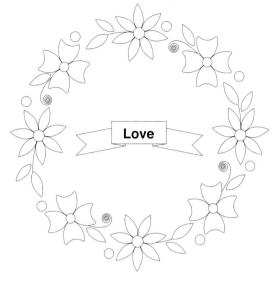

Valentine's Day, page 54

Happy Birthday II, page 60

Happy Birthday I, page 55

Memories of Spring, page 57

Actual size

Snowflake 1, page 84

Snowflake 4, page 86

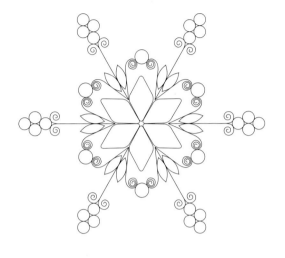

Snowflake 5, page 87

Christmas Poinsettia and Candles, page 82

Actual size

Snowflake 3, page 86

Snowflake 2, page 85

Christmas Square Wreath
with Poinsettia and Bells, page 80

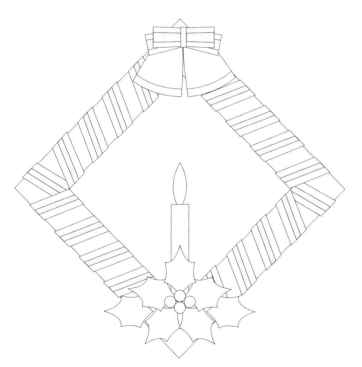

Christmas Spiral Wreath with Bells, page 83

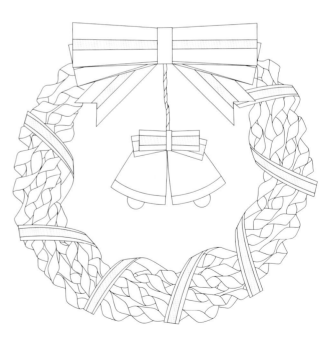

80% of actual size

Flower Wreath, page 95

Flower and Bee, page 96

Potpourri Gift Sachets

Actual size

Flowers and a Butterfly, page 99

Bouquet, page 94

May Roses, page 97

Wildflowers,
page 98

Place Cards

Actual size

Blue Marquise Flowers, page 111

Turquoise Marquise Flower and
Grape Teardrop Flowers, page 110

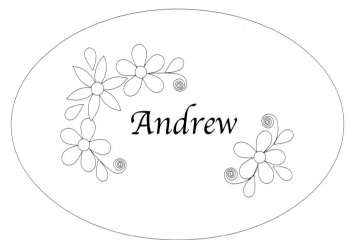

Purplish Blue Marquise Flower and
White Teardrop Flower, page 106

Pink Roses and Purple Teardrop Flowers, page 109

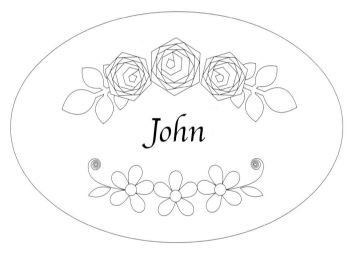

Pink Rose and White Flowers, page 107

Lavender and Purplish Blue Teardrop Flowers, page 108

Potpourri Sachet, page 91

85% of actual size

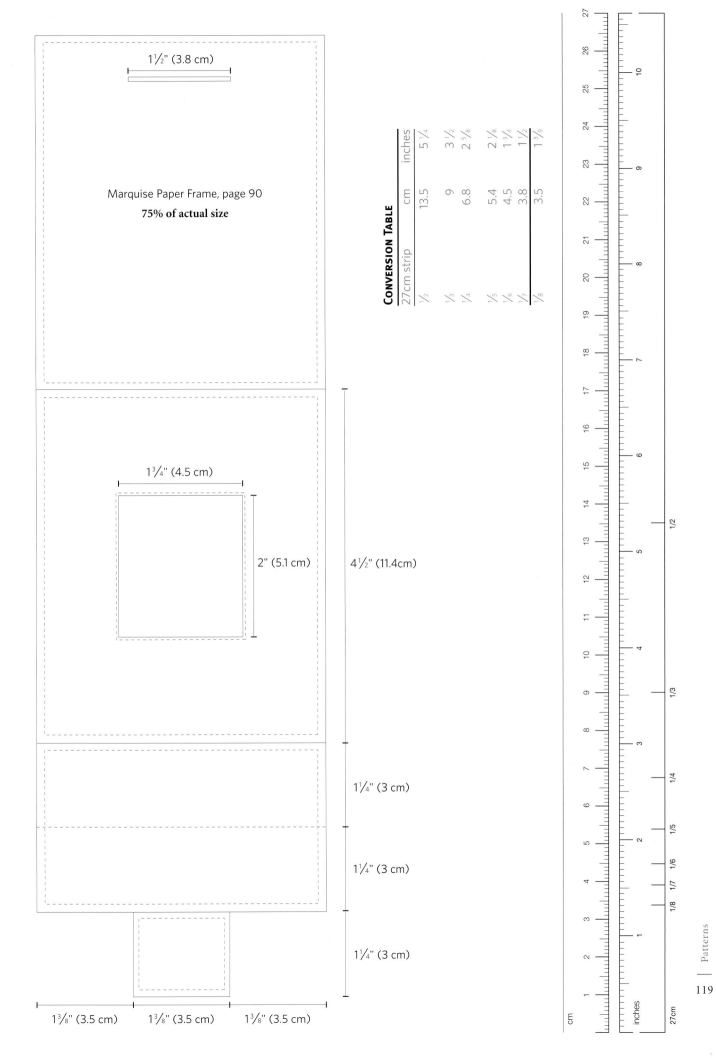

1½" (3.8 cm)

Marquise Paper Frame, page 90

75% of actual size

1¾" (4.5 cm)

2" (5.1 cm)

4½" (11.4cm)

1¼" (3 cm)

1¼" (3 cm)

1¼" (3 cm)

1⅜" (3.5 cm)   1⅜" (3.5 cm)   1⅜" (3.5 cm)

CONVERSION TABLE

27cm strip	cm	inches
½	13.5	5 ¼
⅓	9	3 ½
¼	6.8	2 ⅝
⅕	5.4	2 ⅛
⅙	4.5	1 ¾
⅐	3.8	1 ½
⅛	3.5	1 ⅜

Gallery of
Paper Quilling Art

A Flower Meets a Butterfly

Subtle floral fragrance, the flapping of butterfly wings, and the trembling of tree branches are felt through the paper. Nature provides endless inspiration and color for paper quilling.

(Top) Size: 17" × 17" (43 × 43 cm)

(Bottom) Size: 19¾" × 19¾" (50 × 50 cm)

Tree I

Size: 13¾" × 13¾" (35 × 35 cm)

Tree II

Size: 13¾" × 13¾" (35 × 35 cm)

Harmony of Wildflowers

Size: 21¾" × 15¾" (55 × 40 cm)

Wildflowers

Size: 18" × 15" (46 × 38 cm)

Patterns

Size: 19¾" × 11¾" (50 × 30 cm)

Waving in the Breeze

Size: 15¾" × 11¾" (40 × 30 cm)

This quillwork creates the sensation of the subtle movements of slender stems and small blossoms. Narrow, delicate paper strips convey the encounter between wildflowers and breeze.

Claire Sun-ok Choi

Claire Sun-ok Choi was born in Seoul, South Korea, and studied early childhood education in college. She is a member of the North American Quilling Guild and the Quilling Guild (UK), and works as a paper quilling crafter and card designer in Vancouver, Canada. As a devoted paper quiller, she spreads the beauty of quilling by creating and exhibiting exquisite artwork using this delicate technique.

In 2000, she held her first solo exhibition, Paper Wanting to Be Flowers. In 2002, 2004, and 2007, she participated in group exhibitions at the Ferry Building Gallery in Vancouver. In 2005 and 2006, she received the Best-Quilled Works award of the North American Quilling Guild, and in 2006 received two Best-Quilled Works awards of the Quilling Guild (UK).

She is the author of *Designing Handcrafted Cards* (Quarry, 2004).